WISDOM
FROM THE
RAMAYANA
ON LIFE AND RELATIONSHIPS

CHAITANYA CHARAN

BEL!EF

Reprint 2022

FiNGERPRINT! BEL!EF
An imprint of Prakash Books India Pvt. Ltd.

113/A, Darya Ganj, New Delhi-110 002,
Tel: (011) 2324 7062 – 65, Fax: (011) 2324 6975
Email: info@prakashbooks.com/sales@prakashbooks.com

facebook www.facebook.com/fingerprintpublishing
twitter www.twitter.com/FingerprintP
www.fingerprintpublishing.com

ISBN: 978 93 8814 482 7

Processed & printed in India

Dedicated to

My many spiritual teachers,

who enriched my appreciation

of the Ramayana

CONTENTS

Introduction

As a speaker on spiritual subjects, I am often given specific topics to talk about. Once I was asked to speak on the Ramayana as Ram Navmi was just round the corner. I wanted to make the class relevant for the audience. And I was especially concerned about two of my friends who had been close to each other, but had recently become alienated because of a misunderstanding.

Somehow I felt inspired to speak the Vali-Sugriva story. I spoke how the two brothers had been the best of friends, but had ended up as mortal enemies—all due to a series of misunderstandings. While speaking, I felt intrigued by the close parallels of that story with the situation on my mind. Later I came to know that those two friends had felt moved by that talk to come together for clarification and reconciliation.

I felt grateful because my talk had emerged without any conscious preparation on my part. But as I journaled about the incident later, I sensed I might be on to something bigger. So I wrote an article on that talk's theme and published it on my website thespiritualscientist.com. When several readers appreciated the article, I felt inspired to write more similar articles. I decided to reread the Ramayana from the perspective of relationships and I discovered a treasure trove hidden in plain sight.

Hidden in Plain Sight

As an Indian, the Ramayana had always been in plain sight for me, being integral to the country's cultural fabric. I was introduced to the Ramayana in my early childhood through the stories told by my grandparents and parents. Right next to our house in Chandrapur, Maharashtra, was a small Hanuman temple, and just behind our house was a Rama temple. When I was in primary school, we relocated to Nasik, the place where Rama had lived during exile. In our house in the bedroom hung a picture of Hanuman carrying a mountain. That picture is one of my foremost memories of the Ramayana. My father, who always provided me with abundant books, gave me *Amar Chitra Katha* issues that depicted various Ramayana stories. When the epic was televised for the first time, I watched it eagerly.

When I was studying engineering, I was introduced to the intellectual depth of the *bhakti* tradition through the writings of my *paramguru* Srila Prabhupada and his followers. I found the wisdom so appealing and fulfilling that I decided to dedicate my life to studying and sharing it. During my studies as a monk, I heard Ramalila narrated by my guru Radhanath Maharaja and was swept in by its sweetness. I also came across the Ramayana retold by Krishna Dharma and was captivated by its vivid visual imagery and linguistic elegance.

But when I stumbled on the relationship-focused perspective for approaching the epic, it came alive for me like never before—its relevance was no longer hidden. Thereafter I re-studied the epic, referring to the original Sanskrit and its translations, those published by Gita press and those available at valmikiramayan.net. I also found illuminating the many commentaries available at valmiki. iitk.ac.in. I scanned through the various retellings of the Ramayana in the Mahabharata, the Puranas, and in the vernacular renditions.

All these studies deepened my appreciation of the Ramayana, especially its eminent relevance.

Relationships—Human and Divine

The Ramayana presents an intriguing blend of human-divine relationships. The name 'Ramayana', which means 'the journey of Rama', is an eponym referring to its central character. While Rama is understood in the bhakti tradition to be God descended to this world in a human form, the Valmiki Ramayana focuses not on his divinity, but on his seeming humanity. Indeed, the seminal question that leads to the unfolding of this original Ramayana is: What are the qualities of an ideal human being? In answering this question, the epic places the divine in the midst of human relationships.

The Ramayana's beauty lies in, among other things, the sweetness and selflessness of the relationships it features. Its central characters exude a timeless charm that has spoken to the hearts of millions for millennia. While the Ramayana's world features some characters that might seem mythical to us now, still they have emotions like ours; they face dilemmas like we do; and they make choices and endure consequences just as we do. Thus, they are more similar to us than they might appear at first.

Our specific situations will be different from those of the Ramayana characters; still, underlying those differences are universal principles that can guide us even today. This classic speaks to us not by asking for replication of everything it depicts, but by inspiring us towards emulation of the timeless principles it demonstrates. By coming to know its characters from this principle-centred perspective, we can come to know ourselves better.

Additionally, reading the Ramayana nourishes our relationship with the supreme divinity, Rama. And as Rama is all-pure, contemplation on him helps free us of the impurities that make us act impulsively, thereby undermining our efforts to improve our relationships.

Our essential self—the soul—is like a precious stone buried under the layers of impure mental impressions. Just as the effulgence of a jewel shines forth once it is excavated and cleaned, similarly, the natural qualities of the soul shine forth when we excavate it from layers of impure impressions and purify ourselves by cultivating devotional impressions. Meditating on the Ramayana offers such purification and thereby helps us to discover moral muscles that we didn't know we had. Thus, reading the Ramayana from the perspective of relationships is immensely empowering. The epic offers not just knowledge about the right action, but also moral strength to act rightly.

I have selected incidents from the Ramayana and presented them within the context of themes important for relationships—judgmentality, harsh speech, anger, suspicion, and arrogance, for example. My purpose here is not so much to narrate the story as to meditate on its relevance. Still, enough of the relevant incidents are described, sometimes using retold dialogues, to provide context for the lessons. For readers unfamiliar with the Ramayana, I have provided a summary of the epic in the first appendix. The Ramayana reflects a worldview centred on bhakti, pure devotional love for God. The second appendix gives an accessible introduction to that worldview.

The bhakti tradition considers the actions of Rama to be *lila*, a word that has no precise English equivalent. Lila connotes actions done for pleasure, something like the roles played in a drama. However, these actions are neither frivolous nor fantastical; they occur eternally in the spiritual arena known as the immortal abode of love and are considered the supreme reality. The words 'play' or 'pastime' are used as approximate English equivalents. I have occasionally used pastime wherever the context necessitated, but have generally preferred more familiar usages such as incident or episode. When the Ramayana is seen as pastime, all the characters therein can be seen as simply acting according to divine will, furthering by their actions the unfolding of a higher plan. Simultaneously, the epic can be seen from an ethical perspective, wherein we analyze its incidents to draw guidelines for decision-making in our life. Though this book focuses on such an analysis of the Ramayana, the purpose is not so much to judge the ethical probity of its characters as to learn life-lessons from their situations, dispositions, and actions.

Each article in this book is complete in itself—it conveys a message that will help you in living a spiritually fulfilling and meaningful life. I have arranged these articles in the sequence in which the corresponding events occur in the Ramayana but the articles can be read in any sequence. Given that each article was written as a stand-alone piece, the book has some repetition, especially in the conclusions. But that repetition may well be a strength, driving home from multiple perspectives the rationale of those concluding points.

I have learnt many lessons from the Ramayana, and those lessons have been deepened by the intense contemplation necessary for writing. I hope and pray that despite my many limitations as a seeker and a student of the Ramayana, this book will assist you in enriching yourself with the epic's wisdom.

— CHAITANYA CHARAN

CHAPTER ONE

Kaikeyi-Manthara:
Devastation by Disinformation

One of the most heart-wrenching events in the entire Ramayana is the conspiracy that led to the exile of Rama. From the devotional perspective, this incident brings forth the exalted spiritual emotion of love in separation. From the cosmic administration's perspective, it triggers the chain of events that culminate in Rama's fulfilling the purpose of his descent—ending Ravana's reign of terror. Simultaneously, from the ethical perspective, this incident illustrates our human vulnerability to disinformation—it shows how even good people can get misled into doing terrible things.

In our culture, many vested interests promote their selfish ends through systematic disinformation campaigns. So, a close look at this Ramayana episode can help us combat disinformation.

A Mission of Manipulation

This story unfolded in the city of Ayodhya, the capital of the kings of the solar dynasty. The reigning monarch, Dasharatha, had ruled virtuously for many years. On seeing his old age approaching, he felt inspired to transfer power to a worthy successor, his oldest son, Rama. To formalize this decision, he called an extended assembly of courtiers and leading citizens from various classes, and conveyed to them his desire to transfer power. The assembly unanimously approved his decision. They resolved that the process for succession begin from the next morning itself.

From this jubilant public setting, the Ramayana's spotlight shifts to a private setting—the inner chambers of the palace of Kaikeyi, Dasharatha's youngest wife. Due to her beauty, Kaikeyi had become the king's favourite queen, displacing his senior-most queen, Kaushalya. Despite the inevitable tensions created by such a power shift, the overall family atmosphere remained cordial. Neither Kaushalya nor Kaikeyi bore any malice towards each other. Their respective sons, Rama and Bharata, as well as their two other siblings, Lakshmana and Shatrughna (sons of an intermediate queen Sumitra), lived in cheerful fraternal amity.

This familial harmony was destroyed in one night

during which a self-interested person launched a mission of manipulation. That dark instigator was an elderly hunchbacked maidservant of Kaikeyi, Manthara. This spinster-schemester wanted to maintain at all costs her privileged position in the royal palace as the favourite maidservant of the king's favourite queen. If Rama became the king, she feared that his mother would become the foremost dowager and Kaikeyi would be relegated to the position of just another member in the royal family. This would downgrade Manthara to the level of just another maidservant. Due to her hunchback, Manthara had sometimes been the butt of friendly jokes. Though such teasing hadn't been malicious, she had resented it bitterly. Such banter had stopped with her ascension to a prominent position in the royal staff. Dreading a return to a position of insignificance and scorn, she decided to use her wiles on Kaikeyi and somehow stop the transfer of power. Let's catch up with the action in the Ramayana in its second book, the Ayodhya-kanda, in the palace of Kaikeyi.

Rushing to Kaikeyi's side with a scowl on her face, Manthara told her, "While you are sitting peacefully, do you know what is happening? Kaushalya's son, Rama, is going to be declared the regent tomorrow."

Kaikeyi's face lit up in joy. "How wonderful! Here is a gift to you for bringing this joyous news." She handed her maid a jewel necklace. Flinging the necklace to the ground and scowling even more, Manthara replied, "Though you are the daughter of a king, how can you be so naïve? Do you not see that this is a scheme to deprive Bharata of power?"

Kaikeyi was used to her maid's sullenness. "Rama is the eldest son. He is entitled to be the next king. Maybe after him, Bharata will become the next king."

Manthara snorted, "After Rama, his son will become the king. Once the kingship passes over to Kaushalya's son, it will never return to you." As Kaikeyi pondered her words, Manthara swooped down on her unsuspecting prey. "If everything had been above board, why the haste to perform this ceremony when Bharata is not here?"

Actually, Bharata's absence was simply a happenstance—he was out-of-station when the king felt an inner call to retire and promptly acted on it. Moreover, Bharata being the youngest son had no claim to the throne, which was meant to go by primogeniture to the oldest son, Rama.

Such facts notwithstanding, Manthara exploited the happenstance of Bharata's absence to sow a seed of suspicion in Kaikeyi's heart. And then she watered that seed well into the night with a dystopian tale spun from her imagination:

"Once her son becomes the king, do you think Kaushalya will forget how Dasharatha favoured you over her? No. She will extract revenge by reducing you to her serving maid. And Rama will see Bharata as a threat. Finding some pretext, he will have Bharata arrested, maybe even executed."

By the end of Manthara's diatribe, Kaikeyi became ready to do anything for stopping the 'conspiracy.' Seeing her readiness, her maid suggested, "Do you remember the promise Dasharatha had made to you long ago to grant you two boons? Now is the time to ask for them. Ask that Bharata be designated as the royal heir and that Rama be exiled to the forest for fourteen years."

Wanting that her scheme not fail because of any softheartedness on Kaikeyi's part, Manthara added, "The king will oppose Rama's exile. But don't go soft because of this. As long as Rama is in the kingdom, Bharata will not be accepted by the citizens as the king. Rama needs to be out of the kingdom for a long enough time so that Bharata can win them over."

Hard Heart Breaks Hearts

What followed was a collision between Kaikeyi's heart and Dasharatha's heart. While the king's heart was soft at the prospect of the coronation, his queen's heart had become harder than stone due to believing the conspiracy theory. When their hearts collided, the impact left the king heartbroken.

Late in the night, Dasharatha finished overseeing the arrangements for the ceremony to be held the next day. Wanting to share his joy with his favourite queen, he came to her palace. When she reminded him of his past promise, he unsuspectingly reiterated his commitment to honour that promise. But when he heard her two wishes, he was petrified and collapsed in a swoon. On returning to consciousness, he realized that the nightmare was real. He strove feverishly to deter his wife from her ruthless resolve. Finally, he broke down into piteous tears and fell begging at her feet—both actions utterly uncharacteristic of a monarch. Yet Kaikeyi remained unmoved by her husband's desperate pleas.

Being bound by his word of honour, the king was forced to grant her wishes. But being horrified to see that his loving wife had become an unfeeling ogress, he disowned her. In a voice choked with agony and fury, he declared that with the granting of her wishes, his obligation to her was over, as was his relationship with her.

Despite hearing such a dreadful declaration, Kaikeyi still remained unrelenting. Her heart had become so cold and hard that it had no room left for anything except her scheme: No room for any conjugal affection for her husband. No room for any maternal affection for her stepson, Rama, who had accepted the grievous diktat against him with disarming grace. No room for feminine concern for her daughter-in-law, Sita, who had to don rough tree bark for joining her husband in his exile. No room for respect for the venerable royal priest, Vashishtha, who implored her to desist from such a nefarious plan. And no room for fear of public censure as the shocked courtiers and citizens condemned her.

After Rama departed for the forest, the aggrieved Dasharatha found separation from him unbearable. Even more agonizing was the thought that he himself had sentenced his son to exile. This sentence was reserved for the worst of criminals, being just one level below execution. And he had meted out that brutal sentence to one who had done no wrong, to one whom he should have protected, to one who had been born from his own blood. Crushed by anguish, Dasharatha's broken heart broke down totally— he breathed his last soon after his son's exile. The whole kingdom sank into gloom at this double loss of both their cherished prince and their revered monarch.

The Imaginary Bharata Versus the Real Bharata

Manthara had exploited the fissures between co-wives to set off a catastrophic earthquake. That quake had now given rise to a tsunami that inundated the whole of Ayodhya with agony. Yet not one drop of that ocean touched Kaikeyi's heart. Her transmogrification from wise, kind, and gentle to foolish, cruel, and harsh was unbelievable.

Given that she was not innately evil, how did she justify her horrendous actions to herself? By masking them in the garb of vigilant maternal concern. She imagined that she was doing all this for her son Bharata, who being absent couldn't protect his interests. She believed her maternal rationalization so completely that nothing else mattered to her—no one's words, emotions, or actions could dent her resolve. Yet her justification couldn't but crumble to powder when debunked by the very person it claimed to defend—Bharata.

Kaikeyi's son had anxiously hastened to Ayodhya, being summoned by Vashishtha, who was officiating as the provisional head of state. On arriving in Ayodhya, he saw the once cheery city looking dreary, like a ghost town. Feeling deep misgivings, he rushed to his mother's chambers, expecting to meet both his parents there. On seeing his mother, he offered her his respects and enquired about his father's well-being. Kaikeyi recounted her own version of events, stressing how she had done so much to protect Bharata's right to the kingdom.

Bharata was too sharp to fall for such spin doctoring. Hearing about his father's demise and his brother's exile left him shaken. Hearing that his own mother had caused these calamities left him shattered. Hearing her claiming that she had done all this for his sake left him sickened. He found his mother's words so revolting that he felt sorely tempted to violate the *kshatriya* code that one should not raise one's hand against a woman. Somehow checking himself, he poured his fury out in words. Castigating his unrepentant mother, he deemed her an evil witch born for the destruction of their dynasty.

Kaikeyi heard her son's denunciation with disbelief and dismay. In her imagination, she had fashioned a Bharata who lauded her actions. When the real Bharata condemned those very actions, she realized to her horror that the Bharata who lauded her was nothing more than her imagination. As that imaginary Bharata died a quick death, so did her rationalization. And the monstrosity of what she had done hit her with a force of a thousand thunderbolts. She repented fervently, begging for Bharata's forgiveness. She even went with him to the forest to second his request that Rama return and reclaim the throne. But it was too late—

the juggernaut had already gained a fearsome momentum and nothing, not even its chief pusher, could stop it.

How did Kaikeyi become so misled? By a double blunder—she believed uncritically whatever Manthara told her, and she didn't seek any second opinion. She let herself be so persuaded by just one person's view that she rejected everyone else's advice.

Don't Just Talk *about* Others; Talk *with* Others

As Manthara was for Kaikeyi, we too may have some people who seem to be like our well-wishers, but who end up coming between us and our actual well-wishers. In homes, meddling relatives sometimes come in between affectionate couples. In offices, an envious colleague may similarly come in between a team member and a team leader. By drawing an imaginary line between unconnected events and planting unwarranted suspicions in our heart, such disinformers may paint a grim picture that we will soon be betrayed. Once our paranoia is triggered, we may end up becoming the betrayer, as Kaikeyi became.

When someone casts an aspersion on a loved one, rather than believing the accuser, we need to give the accused a chance to clarify their position. A common blunder we make is that we often talk *about* people instead of talking *with* people. If Kaikeyi had talked with Dasharatha as soon as the doubt had risen in her mind, things would have been amicably clarified and resolved. But instead of talking with Dasharatha, she talked about Dasharatha with Manthara. Or rather she let Manthara talk about him with her. And by hearing uncritically from Manthara, Kaikeyi's suspicion became a conviction—she convicted Dasharatha in the court of her heart without giving him any chance to defend himself. She became the plaintiff, the plaintiff's lawyer, the judge, and the jury all rolled into one. Actually, the reality was worse—she was just a bystander who was persuaded to become a plaintiff and then to give the power of attorney to Manthara. And Manthara acting as the plaintiff's lawyer, the judge, and the jury, convicted Dasharatha as guilty—a verdict that Kaikeyi naïvely accepted.

While it is easy to condemn Manthara and even Kaikeyi, it is more helpful to introspect about times when we ourselves might have acted like them, and how we could have avoided, or at least minimized conflicts by seeking clarifications.

A note of caution: Clarifications need to be sought in a non-accusatory way. If others don't have any inkling of where we are coming from, then our voicing the suspicion itself may hurt them grievously. So, instead of making a value judgment of any kind, we can just present facts and seek explanations. If Kaikeyi had gently asked Dasharatha why he was appointing his successor so hastily in the absence of Bharata, Dasharatha would have explained how he had had jolting reminders of his mortality. And Kaikeyi's apprehensions would have been allayed without her needing to even voice them, leave alone act on them.

In fact, hearing his concern might well have brought her closer to him at a spiritual level as they prepared together to accept the retired order of life.

But instead of seeking clarification, Kaikeyi made a presumption about Dasharatha's motivation, thereby bringing a calamity on the dynasty and on the kingdom at large. Instead of unwittingly bringing a similar calamity in our relationships, we can seek clarification by objectively presenting facts and gently soliciting explanations.

Spiritual Empowerment

As a broader strategy for protecting ourselves from disinformation, we need to strengthen our intellectual and ethical muscles. With stronger intellects, we can penetrate to the actual beyond the apparent, thereby discerning the disingenuity in disinformation. With better ethical muscles, we can resist the promises of quick pleasure that disinformationists dangle to make us lower our guard.

The process of *bhakti-yoga* helps us strengthen both these muscles. Devotional study of scripture sharpens our discerning power and hones our intellectual muscles. Devotional remembrance of the Lord provides a higher inner fulfilment that empowers us to say no to lower temptations.

Unfortunately, disinformation is so pervasive that it can distort our perception of bhakti-yoga too. With a barrage of half-truths and untruths about spirituality and spiritual organizations, disinformation can assault our sacred faith. We can best protect our faith by entirely avoiding such anti-devotional propagandists. But if we somehow hear from them, we shouldn't let their opinions alone determine our spiritual decisions. By seeking clarification from trustworthy spiritual mentors, we can get a balanced understanding that protects our faith in bhakti's potency.

Disinformation threatens us not just externally but also internally. If we compare Ayodhya to our heart, then Manthara is like the mind. The mind comes up with the deadly duo of doubt and desire—doubt paralyzes our devotion and desire aggravates our worldly infatuation. Being misled by the mind, we become like Kaikeyi and exile the Lord from our heart.

To counter the mind's insinuations, we need to meticulously avoid the two mistakes Kaikeyi made. Firstly, we need to avoid hearing the mind uncritically. Unfortunately, the mind is always with us, and it always has the opportunity to spin its self-serving yarn. So, we need to be constantly vigilant. Secondly, if the mind's persuasion starts swaying us from our moral and spiritual principles, we need to counter it with the enlightening voices of sacred texts and their saintly teachers. We can take both these precautions by conscientiously engaging ourselves in bhakti-yoga practice. By such absorbing spiritual engagement, we will pre-empt the mind's misleading stratagems and will instead be led by timeless wisdom towards our all-round well-being.

Rama Leaving Ayodhya: Concern for Others' Distress Minimizes Our Distress

The Ramayana teaches how to respond to adversity with dignity. While many of its characters demonstrate grace amidst duress, Rama demonstrates it most poignantly, especially when he was exiled for no fault of his.

We all face various kinds of problems—persistent problems that we can do nothing about, such as, say, a back-pain; problems that come when we expect trouble; and problems that we don't expect at all. The utterly unexpected problems are especially difficult to respond gracefully to. When we are expecting a pat and get a slap instead, we feel the most hurt.

Similar was the adversity that befell Rama when he was to be enthroned as the prince regent and eventually the king. On the night prior to that joyous celebration, his father Dasharatha was manipulated by his youngest wife, Kaikeyi, into fulfilling two promises he had made long ago. She demanded that Rama be sent to the forest for fourteen years and that her son Bharata be enthroned instead of Rama. Dasharatha was shocked and shattered. But being an honourable king, he had to fulfil his promise to her when she rejected all his desperate pleas to relent.

Early next morning, when Rama came to meet his father before going for the celebration, Kaikeyi coldly informed him of what the king had promised. Since that point, Rama's dealings with various people are exemplary and instructive.

With Kaikeyi

Though the adversity that had befallen him would have been staggering for most people, Rama remained externally composed and became internally contemplative. Seeing that Kaikeyi had become utterly cold-hearted in pursuing her agenda, he decided to try to bring down her animosity by softening her heart. He told her gently, "I had always considered you my mother. I thought that you too had considered me your son. But today I am saddened to know that you never did."

Kaikeyi would have expected this to be a build-up for an argument about her utter unfairness in treating Rama. Just when she would have been preparing to defend and counter, Rama disarmed her, "If you had accepted me as your son, you would have directly asked me for the kingdom instead of having to go to and through my father."

While Kaikeyi was still processing this astounding statement, Rama continued and assured her, "To please you and to honour my father's word, I will soon proceed to the forest."

Thus, knowing that his family would remain in a state of great tension as long as Kaikeyi maintained her hostility towards other family members, Rama tried his best to decrease the tension without reacting impulsively. Trying to decrease the anger of those who have grievously wronged us, at whom we have every right to be angry requires a remarkably selfless level of love.

With Dasharatha

Though his father was the person who had consented to his exile, Rama never blamed him. The Ramayana commentators point out that during this meeting between Dasharatha and Rama, the mortified king could hardly utter a single coherent word—except for calling out Rama again and again, and crying uncontrollably. Seeing his father's agony, Rama tried his best to solace him, "Father, I feel no resentment towards anyone. I will promptly proceed to the forest."

Later, after making all the arrangements for going to the forest, Rama came back to see Dasharatha and take his leave. Then, Dasharatha desperately tried various ways to alleviate the inevitable. He urged Rama, "Stay for just one more day so that I can offer you all royal comforts."

Rama knew that the longer he delayed his departure, the more Kaikeyi would become angry and consequently the more his father would be distressed. He replied gently to his father, "I consider going to the forest to honour your word a privilege. And I don't want to delay it for even one moment."

Love is sometimes conveyed by expressing our emotions and sometimes by concealing them. At the time of farewell from our loved ones, we may feel aggrieved, but if expressing that grief will aggravate their feelings of separation, delay the departure, and thereby jeopardize an important and urgent service, then we need to conceal our emotions. Such keeping our emotions within our heart is a testimony to our love. It demonstrates that our love is not just about our feelings but also about the well-being of our loved ones whose distress we wish to minimize. Rama demonstrated such love in his dealings with Dasharatha.

With Lakshmana

Rama's younger brother was infuriated at the injustice of the command handed out to Rama. Exile was a terrible punishment, second only to the worst of all punishments— execution. Sentencing to exile a person who is totally blameless was outrageous.

Lakshmana urged Rama to protest, even revolt. Going further still, he assured Rama of his full support. His eyes wide and his nostrils flared, seething with anger, he roared, "Anyone who dares to come in the way of your coronation will have to meet my unstoppable arrows."

As he spoke, his anger grew further till it targeted his father. "The king has become blinded by lust for his youngest wife. That's why he has issued such an unjust command."

Rama tried to calm him, "I saw that our father was overwhelmed by sorrow at my exile. He acted not out of infatuation but out of obligation—but he is bound by the promise that he had made to her."

Lakshmana's fury burst out as skepticism, "Who knows if the king was actually obliged. We have never heard about such a promise."

Still remaining calm, Rama reminded him, "All the kings in our line have always honoured their word. Our father too is doing the same, even at great cost to himself. It is our responsibility and privilege to help him maintain that track record of honour."

But Lakshmana was still unconvinced. His temper was boiling and now, he directed it towards Kaikeyi, "She has become heartlessly selfish."

Rama reminded him of past instances of Kaikeyi's love for them—"Her love had been like the flow of the Ganga." Lakshmana retorted, "I can't understand how the Ganga has dried up overnight."

To this, Rama responded, "That's why on seeing the

inconceivable change in her mood, I am convinced him that the will of destiny is being enacted through her."

By bringing destiny into the discussion, Rama tried to deflect Lakshmana's anger away from Kaikeyi, thereby again minimizing the hostility within the family.

Gradually, Rama managed to calm his brother. Though Lakshmana gave up his instinctive desire to lead a coup against the king, he insisted on accompanying Rama to the forest. Rama tried to dissuade him, but Lakshmana remained unrelenting.

Knowing that he had already said no to one of his brother's desires—the desire to resist the sentence of exile—Rama knew that saying no yet again would hurt Lakshmana unbearably. So, he acceded to his request.

With Kaushalya

Kaushalya was devastated on hearing about Rama's imminent exile. When he went to her palace and told her about his exile, she cried out to him:

"First, I suffered a long dark night during which I had been unable to have a son and provide an heir to my husband. Finally, after many difficult vows and austerities, I got you as my son—a son who has fulfilled all my dreams and has become my reason for living. But alas, just when my dream of your coronation is about to come true, things have turned into a nightmare."

What made her misery worse was that this nightmare

had occurred because of the same person who had caused her much distress throughout her married life—her youngest co-wife, Kaikeyi. Though Kaushalya had been the first wife of Dasharatha and had been entitled to the position of the principal queen, that position had been covertly taken away from her by Kaikeyi to whom the king had been far more attracted. Kaushalya had graciously tolerated this slight, but that wound erupted on hearing of Kaikeyi's brazen machinations to deprive Rama and favour Bharata.

Crying piteously, Kaushalya begged Rama, "O Rama, please take me with you to the forest—I won't be able to live with the barrage of insults coming from Kaikeyi. Once Bharata becomes the heir apparent, she will not even try to conceal her insults. And your father will remain silent through it all. If he has sided with her during such a grievous wrong as your banishment, why will he speak out in future?"

Rama commiserated with his mother's plight, but reminded her, "A wife's first duty is to stand by her husband's side through thick and thin." Striving to change her mental picture of her husband from that of a victimizer to a co-victim, Rama told her, "Father is shattered by this turn of events; my exile has happened despite his will. He is devastated at what has happened. To survive this devastation, he will need your moral support, Mother. At this critical juncture, if you too abandon him, that double shock will be unbearable for him."

By thus helping Kaushalya to see things from her

husband's perspective, Rama ensured that their family didn't become further disrupted, either by an overt exodus of many family members to the forest or a covert resentment that might cause it to implode.

Sticking by our loved ones in times of their distress is an enduring test of love. Rama stood by his father and inspired others, including his mother to do the same, even when he could have blamed his father for whatever was happening and got other family members to join him in this blame game. To remove thorns from the path of those who have filled our path with thorns—that is the summit of selfless love.

With Sita

Rama didn't want Sita to suffer because of the calamity that had befallen him. After gently informing Sita about what had happened, he told her how she was to conduct herself in his absence: "I will be leaving for the forest soon. While I am away, O Sita, please don't praise me in the presence of Bharata."

Rama could anticipate possible tensions in the kingdom if Sita praised him in front of Bharata, who would soon be the king. Rama asked her to desist from any such action.

Sita was aghast at what had happened and even more appalled at the prospect of staying alone in the kingdom without her husband. She responded, "O Rama, when my father gave my hand to you in marriage, he told me to stick by your side through thick and thin. I will go with you to the forest."

Rama tried to dissuade her by speaking at length about the many travails of forest life. But Sita remained firm. "The dangers of the forest will be a joy if they provide me your company. Without you, the palace will give me no comfort." When Rama still refused, she resorted to a last, surefire weapon—attacking Rama's masculinity: "Alas, my father has given my hand to a man who doesn't have the courage or the confidence to protect me."

Rather than taking offense at this attack of his virility, Rama saw it as it was intended—an expression of Sita's unshakeable resolve to accompany him to the forest.

He smiled and told her, "O Sita, now I am convinced that you truly want to come with me, that you will find staying in the kingdom more distressing than living in the forest. You are welcome to join me. I will be comforted and delighted to have your company during my stay in the forest."

With Courtiers

As the courtiers and citizens expressed their resentment at the cruelty of Rama's exile, Rama pacified them. "I see no cruelty, only opportunity—the opportunity to please my step mother, who was just like my birthmother; the opportunity to ensure that my father's name will be included in the glorious list of honourable kings who were ready to sacrifice their everything for a higher cause; the opportunity to have my younger brother, who is very dear to me, enthroned as the king; and the opportunity to associate constantly with forest sages and enrich myself with their spiritual wisdom."

By thus amazingly recasting his situation as auspicious instead of inauspicious, Rama helped free the courtiers and citizens from resentment towards their king, thereby preventing any negative effect on the kingdom's administration.

Shifting Our Focus

In our life, when we face distress, we often tend to feel sorry for ourselves and to speak about our sorry state to others. We often lash out at those who we feel have caused us distress. The more we speak about our sad plight, the more we become radiators of distress.

Of course, sharing our troubles can sometimes unburden us, especially when we do so among those who can understand and strengthen us. However, even during such sharing, we may end up wallowing in self-pity—something that only aggravates our feeling of being victimized and makes others feel increasingly troubled.

The preceding analysis is not to minimize or trivialize the problems we face in life—they are often real and serious. And they frequently need tangible solutions that have to be practically implemented. Simultaneously, all problems have a mental component that can make them seem far bigger than what they actually are. We can minimize the mental expansion of our problems by shifting our focus from ourselves to others, from the problems we are facing to the problems that they are facing. This shift of focus helps us keep our sense of perspective and act maturely.

Gita wisdom helps in this shift of focus by reminding us that this world is a place of distress for everyone—all that varies is the form and frequency of distress. Further, all of us can find relief by taking shelter of our Lord and acting in a mood of service to help each other in our spiritual growth. By thus seeing the universality of suffering instead of obsessing over our specific suffering, we can escape the trap of self-pity and progress towards tackling problems instead of perpetuating or aggravating them.

When faced with problems, problems that seem to originate from specific people but which actually are intrinsic to the very fabric of this world, we can meditate that during our life journey, we are not here to see through each other; we are here to see each other through.

CHAPTER THREE

Rama-Lakshmana:
Fatalism or Pragmatism?

Eastern thought is sometimes deemed fatalistic, as holding that everything is predetermined by our past actions and thus leaving little room for human initiative. While Indian literature is filled with diverse thoughts—some of which may be fatalistic— the bhakti literature, which is among the most influential Indian literature, offers a far more nuanced and empowering outlook to life.

Ancient Echoes of Modern Concerns

The Ramayana features an emotionally and intellectually riveting conversation about the interplay of destiny and human initiative.

This conversation occurred at one of the epic's defining moments—when Rama, who was about to be crowned as prince regent, was instead sentenced to forest exile for fourteen years.

While Lakshmana was outraged by the injustice of Rama's exile, Rama calmly responded that he considered his exile the will of destiny and so intended to accept it.

If some of us find Rama's deference to destiny too docile, we may be intrigued to know that so did Lakshmana. Rather than ascribe Rama's exile to destiny, he sought to lay the blame on the human actors involved—Kaikeyi's scheming and, more importantly, the king's complicity. He alleged that the king had become infatuated with his beautiful wife and so had abandoned his duty to protect his own son. To Rama's deference to destiny, the incensed Lakshmana countered that only the impotent accepted injustice passively as the will of destiny; the strong fought injustice to protect their rights—and the kingdom was Rama's right. Lakshmana's arguments may make us feel that his is an intriguingly modern voice railing against the fatalism prevailing in those times.

Seeing through the Stereotype of Fatalism

Significantly, Rama was not fatalistic, as was evident from his dynamic response to other adversities such as the abduction of his wife, Sita. He didn't passively accept her abduction as an act of destiny. When she was abducted, he had no guards, servants, or royal resources for finding her. He could well have seen his destitute condition as the arrangement of destiny and passively accepted Sita's abduction. But the thought of such passivity didn't even cross his mind.

To the contrary, he always discharged his duty of protecting her actively, even proactively. Throughout their stay in the forest, he always ensured that either he or his brother were at hand to protect Sita. And the moment he discovered that she was missing and found signs of a scuffle that pointed to her abduction, he immediately started searching for her. To rescue her, he formed an unlikely alliance with monkey forces, marched hundreds of miles through difficult terrain, and fought against a formidable foe who had bested even the gods.

If Rama responded to Sita's abduction so resourcefully, even forcefully, then why did he accept his own exile so passively? If he didn't ascribe Sita's abduction to destiny, why did he ascribe his own banishment to destiny? Because the defining decider of his responses was the consideration of not destiny, but duty. For Rama as a husband, the protection of his wife was his prime duty, and he didn't even consider abandoning that duty in the name of destiny, no matter how difficult that duty was. For Rama as a son, obedience to his father was his prime duty—a duty he did even if it required renouncing his right to the kingdom.

So, the Ramayana's message is not that we passively give in to destiny, but that we gallantly stick to duty. And if in the course of duty, some inconceivable calamity strikes, we can attribute it to destiny, and continue to do our duty.

An agrarian analogy can illumine this point. For farmers, plowing the field is the duty, whereas the occurrence of timely rains is destiny. Both are needed for a good harvest. Destiny determines whether the plowing will yield harvest, but it doesn't determine whether the farmers plow or not. If they don't plow, then even if the destiny is favourable, rains will cause the growth of weeds, not crops. Significantly, this understanding of the dynamics of duty and destiny is empowering. It offers impetus to do duty even when destiny is unfavourable. Though the farmers may get no harvest when destiny is unfavourable, still their diligent performance of duty will create positive karmic credits that will contribute to their benign future destiny. After all, our destiny is formed not by some unknown arbitrary force, but by our own actions; the accumulated karmic reactions to our past actions in this and previous lives comprise our present destiny. Just as our present destiny is shaped by our past actions, our future destiny is shaped by our present actions.

So, our doing our duty in the present, even when it doesn't produce any result immediately, doesn't go in vain. It comprises good karma and thereby contributes to the congenial destiny that will bring good results in future.

Duty Comprises the Best Response to Destiny

While the relationship between free will and destiny is complex, it can be summed in this broad principle—what happens to us is destiny, how we respond to it is our free will. And we can choose the best response by sticking to our duty.

Here it's important to note the different connotations of the word 'duty.' Nowadays, the word is often used in the sense of a burden, something that one is expected to do or something that has to be done. So if someone exhibits stellar qualities and does something extraordinary, we laud it as 'going beyond the call of duty.' In the bhakti tradition, 'duty' is often the translation of the Sanskrit concept of dharma, which refers to activities that help us achieve our latent potential. By acting according to dharma, we help bring out the best within us—our godly, spiritual side. Doing one's duty, in this sense, is not about stoically carrying a burden allotted by externals, but about resourcefully bringing out one's inner potential by making scripturally-guided choices.

Continuing with this burden-free connotation of 'duty', the highest duty, the *para-dharma*, is that of pure love, *kevala* bhakti. The various interactions among the Ramayana characters can at one level be seen as reciprocations of such spiritual love. But at another level, for our own edification, their actions can be seen as demonstrating principles for choosing the right course of action. When seen in this edificatory sense, the Ramayana demonstrates not resignation to destiny, but dedication to duty as the best means of using our free will.

To further understand how destiny relates with free will, consider, as an analogy, a card game. Destiny determines the hand we get, but we determine how we use it. Claiming that there's no such thing as destiny is like claiming that we have full control over the hand we get—patently untrue. In the game of life, we all get different hands; we are all born with different sets of talents and resources, and throughout our life we face different challenges. Duty as understood in the sense of dharma enables us to make the best use of this hand.

For Rama as an obedient son, his duty was to serve his father. He would normally have done so by accepting the post of prince regent and eventually of the king. But when extraordinary circumstances conspired to have him banished, he stuck to his duty, albeit in a drastically different form—not as a prince, but as an ascetic. And he attributed those extraordinary factors that changed his circumstances to destiny. Inconceivable, inexorable destiny had moved his stepmother to express such uncharacteristic greed for power.

Rama rejected Lakshmana's call for rebellion not because he was fatalistic and feeble, but because he was resourceful and courageous enough to do his duty even when it was exceptionally difficult. To Lakshmana's charge about the king's motivation, Rama pointed out that their father had acted not because of infatuation but because of obligation—he had long ago promised Kaikeyi two boons and was honour-bound to grant them, even when doing so caused him heartbreaking agony. Rama stressed that the king's readiness to keep his word demonstrated not his weakness but his truthfulness.

Rights Don't Trump Responsibilities

Rama's refusal to seize his right to the kingdom by sacrificing his responsibility as a son is instructive. Though something may be our right, it may not always be right for us to claim it. Considerations of our rights need to be balanced with deliberations on our responsibilities. We live in a culture that frequently champions rights and downplays responsibilities. Parents often find it extremely difficult to raise children who feel that they are entitled to things without feeling that they need to do anything to get them.

John F Kennedy's exhortation, "Ask not what your country can do for you—ask what you can do for your country," was a call to shift the focus from rights to responsibilities. Such a shift comes much easier when we have a spiritual conception of life, when we understand ourselves to be souls, and see life from a multi-life perspective wherein results for dutifulness are guaranteed, even if not in this life.

When we are faced with problems, we can deal with them better if we approach them with a positive attitude, focusing, for example, on how the glass is half-full, not half-empty. Illustrating how spiritual wisdom engenders positive outlook, Rama responded to his banishment by stating that he didn't see any cause for distress. He had the satisfaction of ensuring that his father's word is honoured; he had the joy of facilitating the enthronement of his younger brother, who was like a son to him; and he had the opportunity for spiritual growth by the association of sages in the forest, an opportunity that he would otherwise have got only towards the end of his life when he retired to the forest. Thus, Rama's spiritual vision grants him extraordinary positivity. He accepts the adversity of banishment not with hand-wringing and teeth-grinding, but with dignity and determination, looking to make the best of the situation.

That Rama ascribed the adversity that befell him to destiny is significant because he, being God himself, is the Lord of destiny. But he had descended as an avatar not so much to demonstrate his supremacy as to demonstrate the life of an ideal human being. And he did so by exemplifying how to respond to adversity with maturity. If we focus too much on our rights, we may end up beating our head against a wall, trying in vain to get things which we think are our right but which have been taken away by unchangeable circumstances—by the will of destiny. On the other hand, if we focus too much on destiny, we may end up doing nothing at all, thereby depriving ourselves of our authentic rights and letting the world walk all over us. Acceptance of destiny is not a recipe for sentencing oneself to weakness and helplessness; it is the pathway for the most constructive channeling of our energies.

To conclude, the bhakti literature teaches not fatalism but pragmatism—the sound practical intelligence that refuses to buy the lie that everything is in our control. By remembering that there is much we cannot control, pragmatism urges us to focus our energy on those things that we can control.

Nowadays many people suffer from depression, inferiority complex, and suicidal urges. A major reason for such psychological problems is an underlying misconception about controllership: people are led to believe that they can control everything and when they can't control things, they think that something is intrinsically wrong with them and sink into self-flagellating thought patterns. That's why a proper understanding of destiny can be salutary; it can prevent dissipation of our energy in fruitless fantasies or lamentations, and can channelize it towards growth-inducing choices.

CHAPTER FOUR

Dasharatha-Kaikeyi: Doomed by Destiny or Desire?

What do we do when a promise we have given comes back to strangle us? What do we do when a loved one whom we have implicitly trusted acts like our worst enemy? What do we do when, at the very moment our dearest dreams are meant to come true, they turn into nightmares?

The Ramayana narrates how these questions confronted Dasharatha, the reigning monarch of Ayodhya, when his plans for succession were disastrously derailed.

The Devastating Demand

Kaikeyi was a heroic wife worthy of a great king—she had saved her husband's life. Once, when the king was engaged in a deadly war with demonic forces, his charioteer was slain and he himself was knocked unconscious. With fearless presence of mind, Kaikeyi grabbed the reins and steered his chariot to safety. Feeling astounded and indebted, he gave her two boons, promising that he would provide whatever she desired.

Being incited by Manthara, Kaikeyi decided to use those boons to fulfil her designs. When Dasharatha approached her that night, she placed herself in a dishevelled condition in the sulking chamber. Concerned at what was afflicting his favourite wife, the king got carried away by his desire to pacify her. Not knowing what Kaikeyi was going to ask and being elated at the upcoming elevation of his dear son, Rama, he unwittingly promised to fulfil her request, and promised thrice in the name of Rama. Little did he know that he was like an ignorant animal entering a fatal trap.

Kaikeyi asked that Rama be banished to the forest for fourteen years and in his place, Bharata be installed as the prince regent. On hearing Kaikeyi's demands, he was stunned, shocked, shattered. Not even in his wildest dreams had he thought that she would ask for something like this. Desperately, he begged her to relent, even falling at her feet. But Kaikeyi's heart had turned to stone. The next morning, she summoned Rama and informed him that the king had ordered that he be banished.

Trapped between Promise and Plan

Had Dasharatha erred in making a blanket promise? Possibly, but not necessarily. He had no reason to suspect Kaikeyi—she had treated Rama like her own son and had shown no resentment at his being groomed as the heir apparent. When she made her demands, the principled monarch was torn between two duties—the duty of honouring his word to his wife and the duty of giving his son his due legacy.

On hearing Kaikeyi's words, Rama took the news stoically and gracefully agreed to obey his father's command. Actually, Dasharatha never spoke that Rama be exiled; it was Kaikeyi who spoke those unconscionable, unbearable words on the king's behalf. And the mortified king watched on mutely, crying and swooning to see the horror unfolding before his eyes.

Rama entrusted his affairs to others, readied himself for departing to the forest, and came to his father, "O venerable father, to honour your word, I am now ready to leave for the forest. Please give me your blessings."

Seeing him, Dasharatha became frantic with anxiety, and said, "O Rama, please don't go to the forest." Desperately straining to think of some way to stop the impending exile, he told Rama, "I am an unworthy king. Please stage a coup, overthrow and imprison me, and take the throne. Then you won't have to go to the forest."

Of course, Rama declined, politely yet categorically: "O father, may you rule for many more years. After returning from the forest, I look forward to resuming my service to you." Offering his respects to his father, he turned and departed. Dasharatha watched on, helpless.

We may wonder: Was a king's sense of honour so important as to be worth the exile of one's own son? Yes. The sense of honour ensured that monarchs wouldn't abuse the considerable power at their command. Having it bred into them since childhood that a person's worth was only as much as the worth of their word, they were thus trained to use power for honourable purposes. Though Dasharatha had planned to honourably hand the kingdom's reins to Rama, he was thwarted because of his word of honour to his wife.

Unavoidable Reaction to Unintentional Action

After Rama's departure, Dasharatha could do nothing except think of Rama and call out his name in dejection. When his first wife, Kaushalya, tried to console him, he told her a distressing incident from his past.

Long ago, he had accidentally killed a young man whom he had mistaken to be an animal drinking water in a desert.

Dasharatha had been out hunting, which was a means by which the kings kept the population of animals, especially predators, under control. Also, through hunting, the kings practised the skill of archery and desensitized themselves to the sight of blood and gore. Such desensitization helped them face the brutality of war unflinchingly. As the martial guardians of society, they had to be trained to fight when necessary for protecting the law-abiders from the law-breakers.

During this hunting expedition, Dasharatha had been practising the skill of shooting targets that could only be heard, not seen. Rulers needed this skill to fight at night with devious enemies who didn't respect the martial code that wars be fought only during the day, or who attacked mystically using invisible weapons.

Concealed in a thicket near a river, Dasharatha lay in wait for animals that would come to drink water. On hearing the sound of water being lapped up, he shot an arrow in that direction with lightning speed and heard the sound of the arrow thudding into a target. His satisfaction turned into horror, however, when he heard a human scream. He rushed to the riverside and found a hermit boy lying there.

Wincing in pain and realizing that he was about to die, the boy decided that he had no time to waste in blaming his aggressor. Seeing the remorse on the face of the king, he said, "O king, I had come here to fetch water for my blind parents. They have no one other than me to take care of them. Please take some water for them." Speaking these words, right before Dasharatha's appalled eyes, the boy left his body.

His heart heavy with mountainous remorse, Dasharatha carried the body and the water to Shravan's parents. When he approached them, they sensed by the sound of his movements that he was not their son. When they asked about his identity, the king tearfully told them what had happened.

On hearing that their son was no more, the aged couple was aghast. Shravan's father somehow pulled himself together and performed his son's last rites, with due assistance from a remorseful Dasharatha. Overcome by grief, Shravan's parents couldn't live much longer after their son's death.

Before dying, Shravan's father said to Dasharatha, "Just as I am dying in the agony of separation from my son, you too will one day die in the agony of separation from your son."

Despite being cursed, Dasharatha felt no anger towards the dying father. He knew that he had erred grievously in inadvertently killing a citizen whom he was duty-bound to protect.

As that incident had happened many years ago, it had slipped out of Dasharatha's mind. But after Rama's banishment, when Dasharatha was trying to make sense of things, the curse returned to his mind. At one level, that recollection filled him with illumination, helping him see a pattern amidst the adversities that had just befallen him. At another level, the recollection filled him with resignation, as he realized that destiny was taking its due course, a course that would lead to his death.

Diligence to Duty amidst Deference to Destiny

This Ramayana narrative, along with the flashback, raises several critical questions about the course of human affairs—Are certain things destined to happen? Are we just puppets in the hands of destiny that makes us dance as per its will?

The Ramayana may seem to support this idea. After he was exiled, Rama invoked destiny repeatedly while pacifying others. When Lakshmana railed against the unfairness of Dasharatha's order, Rama calmed him by saying that it was all the will of destiny. Later, when Bharata came to meet him in the forest, Rama told Bharata to bear no animosity towards Kaikeyi, for she had simply acted as destiny had willed.

Reiterating this line of reasoning, the Ramayana states that the mind of Manthara, and thereby of Kaikeyi, was influenced by the gods who wanted Rama to leave Ayodhya and go to the forest to confront the cannibalistic demons there. Through the ensuing encounter, he would rid the world of demonic forces. And indeed, that's how things turned out.

Why did the gods want Rama to leave Ayodhya? To fulfil his mission as a descent of the divine. Rama being supreme is the Lord of destiny too—destiny acts according to his will. That means Rama was exiled by his own will.

However, the Ramayana doesn't stress Rama's divinity—it focuses on his being the ideal human being. And Rama's actions are instructive in understanding how to respond to destiny. Despite repeatedly referring to destiny, neither Rama nor the other characters in the epic act as if they are puppets, pulled helplessly into doing particular things. When faced with perplexities, they reason conscientiously to determine their dharma, the right course of action for them. They draw insights from scripture and tradition, and use their intelligence for applying those insights to their particular situations.

Thus, the characters simultaneously acknowledge destiny and deliberate dharma. Destiny connotes forces beyond our control, and dharma connotes actions that we are meant to choose, implying that those choices are in our control. How can considerations of destiny and duty—of factors beyond our control and factors in our control—be reconciled? By seeing destiny and duty as complementary, not contradictory, as Rama did.

In the third chapter of this book, we discussed how Rama's placid acceptance of his exile was not fatalistic, but pragmatic. Nowadays, we often rebel against any notion of predestination, any idea of resignation to any power higher than human. But just as in Rama's case, Dasharath's surrender to his destiny is not fatalistic either. He tried his best to avert the calamity. Only when nothing worked did he share the story of his being cursed to explain that the adversity had been pre-ordained. The Ramayana gives no indication that any fatalistic sense of predestination decreased his efforts to change Kaikeyi's mind.

The thrust of the Ramayana's discussions is that we not see the events happening in our life as isolated incidents—they are manifestations of a complex chain of factors, a chain into which we implicated ourselves by our past actions. Such a philosophically informed vision helps us respond to reversals intelligently, not impulsively, so that we can act to mitigate the situation, not aggravate it.

From Destiny through Duty to Liberty

Such level-headed pragmatism in the face of destiny is the most empowering option in a disempowering situation. And it becomes even more empowering when coupled with the spiritual practice of bhakti-yoga. This is evident in Dasharatha's actions.

Though deeply afflicted by separation from Rama and though confronted with the inevitability of his own imminent demise, Dasharatha didn't become resentful or hateful towards hostile destiny. He saw the calamity as a reaction to his own past action. Of course, in his particular case, that culpable action had been perpetrated in that very life and he could recollect it. In most cases, we may not be able to recollect the relevant past action, for it may have been done in some previous life. Nonetheless, the key point is that destiny is not arbitrary or inimical; it is orderly and reactional. It gives us reactions to our own past actions.

Accepting the inviolable will of destiny, Dasharatha absorbed himself in the remembrance of Rama. The Ramayana embodies a dynamic, ecstatic tension in

Dasharatha's mind over Rama's identity—is Rama human or divine? The king is told repeatedly by sages that his son is the Supreme Lord descended to this world, and hearing about his son's divinity delights him. Still, that knowledge never became the defining basis of his relationship with Rama. Out of his paternal affection, he saw Rama as his own son, to be protected and provided for by him.

Srimad-Bhagavatam, a pre-eminent bhakti text, declares that absorption in the Lord is always auspicious. If such absorption is continued till the moment of death, it can grant liberation, transporting one to the Lord's eternal abode.

Dasharatha became absorbed in Rama, in a mood of parental affection and intense separation. Thus absorbed, he left his mortal frame and attained reunion with Rama in his supreme abode. The destiny that had brought him such agony ultimately led him to liberation.

And a similar auspicious result happened for the world at large—Rama freed it from the scourge of demonic forces. Intriguingly, destiny's ways turned out to be auspicious for the demons too. Not all of them were innately, incorrigibly evil—they were just led by a fiendish pack of leaders headed by the lecherous Ravana. Rama eliminated those rogue leaders and entrusted the demons' leadership to the virtuous Vibhishana, who brought auspiciousness into the demons' lives.

If we too respond to adverse destiny by sticking to our dharma and absorbing ourselves in our Lord, destiny's ultimate benevolence will eventually become manifest.

CHAPTER FIVE

The Four Brothers: Elevating Our Emotions

Our heart is capable of both noble and ignoble emotions. How we can cultivate higher emotions and curb lower emotions is demonstrated in the Ramayana through the interactions between the two pairs of inseparable brothers: Rama-Lakshmana who are together in exile, and Bharata-Shatrughna who are together in Ayodhya.

Anger Triggered by Suspicion

Rama, Lakshmana, and Sita started living in the forest of Chitrakuta. One day they heard the sounds of an approaching army. At Rama's behest, Lakshmana climbed atop a tree to identify the visitors and recognized Bharata at their forefront. Lakshmana, while serving Rama in the forest, was still angry to see that his brother, who should have been enjoying royal opulence, was instead enduring Spartan austerity in the forest. When he climbed atop a tall tree and saw Bharata coming with a huge army, he thought the worst of him. With his eyes turning red, he returned to Rama's side and said, "That wicked Bharata is in cahoots with his mother. He has brought the army to kill you so that he can get the kingdom for not just fourteen years but for life." Raising his bow in fury, he roared, "He will see my might today. Single-handedly, I will slay him and anyone else who dares threaten you."

Remaining calm, Rama placed his hand gently on Lakshmana's shoulder and replied, "O Lakshmana, do you not remember Bharata's affection for me? I consider it equal to your affection for me." Continuing to calm Lakshmana, Rama said, "I think Bharata is mortified at his mother's intrigues and has come to return the kingdom to me."

Seeing that Lakshmana was still furious, Rama asked, "O Lakshmana, why are you mad at Bharata? Has he offended you in any way? If so, please forgive him, for we all are brothers. Or is it that the forest austerities have made you irritable? Is that why you are resenting Bharata, who is enjoying the royal luxuries that you are missing? If that's the case, I will ask Bharata to exchange places with you—he will stay in the forest with me, and you can enjoy Ayodhya's royal comforts."

Being so gently yet strongly reproached, Lakshmana

felt embarrassed and fell silent. And his embarrassment at his misjudgment increased manifold when he saw Bharata's devotion—how Bharata fervently beseeched Rama to take the kingdom and finally carried Rama's sandals on his head.

Later, after the departure of the visitors from Ayodhya, Lakshmana introspectively asked Rama, "Why am I so short-tempered?" Rama replied, "Because you are an emotional person." Perplexed, Lakshmana asked, "Are emotions undesirable?" Rama answered, "No, not at all. Emotions are the ornaments of life. But we need to choose the emotions that bring out our higher side, not our lower side."

Anger Triggered by Cruelty

How to choose emotions thus is illustrated in an interaction between the other two brothers, Bharata and Shatrughna. This incident occurred before they go to the forest to meet Rama.

The two brothers were returning to their palace after having performed the funeral rites for their deceased father. Bharata, being the de facto head of state, was accosted by a city official about some administrative work. Shatrughna moved on towards the palace and caught sight of Manthara. This scheming maid of Kaikeyi was the root of the conspiracy that led to the exile of Rama and the death of their father. Seeing her dressed in finery—evidently the rewards for successfully masterminding the conspiracy—

Shatrughna felt his blood boil, and he rushed forward to catch her. On seeing Shatrughna and his expression, Manthara turned pale and fled towards Kaikeyi's palace. But the doorkeeper, who like most residents of Ayodhya, was incensed at the conspiracy, grabbed Manthara and handed her to Shatrughna, who shook her violently in fury. The wicked maid shrieked in mortal fear, calling for her mistress. Kaikeyi rushed out and commanded Shatrughna, "Stop. Release her." But the infuriated prince paid her no attention—the anger that had been burning within him for days now rushed forth unchecked.

Fearful of her stepson's uncontrollable wrath, Kaikeyi looked around for help and saw her son, Bharata, approaching. She rushed to him, pleading to him, "O Bharata, please tell Shatrughna to stop." Turning coldly away from her, Bharata addressed Shatrughna, "Stop, O brother. I too have felt the strong impulse to do what you are doing—and do it not just to Manthara, but also to mother." While Kaikeyi heard aghast, Bharata continued, "I restrained that impulse by remembering that giving in to it will displease the very person whom we want to please—Rama. If we hurt Mother or Manthara, Rama will surely be disappointed with us, and whatever chance we have of getting him to return from the forest will be lost." Struck by this thought, Shatrughna released Manthara, who fled to Kaikeyi's arms. And the two brothers walked on towards their palaces, discussing how they could best persuade Rama to return.

Thus, for Bharata and Shatrughna, what mattered

most was who they were angry for, not who they were angry with. They countered the lower emotion of anger by holding on to the higher emotion of love for Rama. For all of us too, cultivating such higher emotions is vital for freeing ourselves from our lower emotions.

Indeed, human culture is meant to provide an environment wherein higher emotions can be nourished and lower emotions countered. Unfortunately, contemporary culture is increasingly doing the opposite, as can be seen, for example, in the advertisement industry.

Deliberate Triggering of Lower Emotions

Advertisements are so ubiquitous today that we may not realize that human society lived without them for millennia. No doubt, people have always promoted their products, but such promotion was never a whole industry, and certainly not a multi-billion-dollar industry. The advertising behemoth took birth soon after the industrial revolution gained steam in the eighteenth and nineteenth centuries. Once goods started being mass produced, promoting them became a big part of the economy and the culture at large. Ads can conceivably help us by informing us about useful products, but that's not the intent behind most ads nowadays. Till the end of the nineteenth century, ads usually focused on the qualities of the products, thereby appealing to customers' intelligence. But then came Sigmund Freud with his ideas about human psyche.

One of Freud's observations was that far stronger than our rationality is our emotionality. To understand this observation, we can compare our rational intelligence to a small raft and our irrational emotions to the waves in a vast turbulent ocean. People can be exhorted to do the right thing by appealing to their rationality. But if something triggers their irrational emotions, it can easily overpower their intelligence, as waves can overturn a raft. Being driven by such emotions, people end up doing terrible things, against their own better intelligence.

The bhakti tradition will see here rough parallels with the concept of the three modes of material nature—goodness, passion, and ignorance. These modes comprise a framework for analyzing the nature of things, especially in terms of their psychological effects on us. The rational faculty correlates with the higher mode of goodness. This mode, the Bhagavad-gita (18.30) states, illumines us with the intelligence to discern what should be done and what shouldn't be done. The irrational emotions correlate with the lower modes of passion and ignorance. These modes impel us to act on the spur of the moment, neglecting warnings from others as well as from our own intelligence.

Actually, the irrational emotions don't exactly destroy the rational intelligence; they subordinate and misappropriate it for their own purposes. Consequently, those under the grip of such emotions often exhibit intelligence, but that intelligence rationalizes and increases their irrational emotions instead of restraining them. History demonstrated this in Nazi Germany's misuse of cutting edge scientific advances in fields, such as eugenics, to irrationally victimize Jews and others in the Holocaust.

This theme of lower emotions hijacking our rational intelligence is seen in the Bhagavad-gita's description of intelligence in the modes of passion and ignorance. We might be inclined to assume that intelligence would correlate with the mode of goodness. Our assumption would be correct, but not complete. The lower modes too feature intelligence, but intelligence abused for unintelligent purposes, being driven by irrational emotions.

Significantly, Gita wisdom also describes a stable state of existence beyond both the ocean and the raft—the state of transcendence. Beyond the three material modes is our pure existence as spiritual beings. We as souls have pure emotions centred on selfless love for God and all living beings in relationship with him. But as the light coming from a white bulb becomes coloured if that bulb is placed in a coloured case, so too the original pure emotions of the soul become distorted due to the coverings of the modes.

When Rama tells Lakshmana to cultivate elevating emotions and avoid degrading emotions, he is essentially telling us to cultivate goodness and transcendence, and avoid passion and ignorance. But the ad industry, using Freud's ideas, does the opposite—or, more precisely, makes us do the opposite.

Advertisers recognized that people could be more forcefully persuaded to purchase products by appealing to their emotions than to their intelligence. So they started using their intelligence to design ads that capitalized on people's irrational emotions.

Torches of Freedom Light the Path to Self-injury

Few things illustrate the deluding power of such advertising as graphically as the 'Torches of Freedom' campaign to make women smoke. This campaign's high point—or rather low point—was the Easter Sunday Parade of 1929 in America. During that parade, many of the leading female icons were paid to smoke cigarettes custom-made for women—cigarettes that were called the 'torches of freedom.' At that time, the women's liberation movement had an immense stronghold on the female imagination. The ad industry exploited this stronghold. By terming cigarettes as 'torches of freedom,' it managed to bag an incredible amount of money by inducing millions of women to smoke not just in America, but also in much of the Western world. Only decades later were the harms of smoking brought to light, especially for women, all the more for pregnant women. Thus, the 'torches of freedom' ended up lighting for millions the road to self-injury.

While most ad campaigns may not be that insidious, still they frequently operate on the same principle of exploiting our emotions. They use human intelligence to trigger human irrationality. Advertisers use their best intelligence based on meticulous research into human psychology to make us crave and slave for their products. Most ads focus not on how good the product is, but on how good the product will make us feel. Thus, advertising becomes pop psychology, which comes streaming into our living rooms through our television sets. By their clever (cunning?) design, ads catch our emotions and thereby our wallets.

And ads are just one of the many things in today's society that exploit us by triggering our lower emotions. To protect ourselves from such emotional manipulation, we need to understand how we can activate and strengthen our higher emotions.

Devotion Brings Out Our Best

Relationships often help us bring out our higher side. Our desire to please the person whom we love inspires us to act properly, thus expressing our higher emotions. And our desire to not displease our loved one empowers us to avoid acting improperly, thus restraining our lower emotions. Of course, this happens only when that person is of basically good character. Otherwise, when we are in bad association, the desire to please others brings out our lower side, as happened in the Mahabharata with Karna because of his desire to please the evil Duryodhana.

In general, when we commit ourselves to a relationship with a good person, that commitment challenges the hold of our lower emotions on us. To the extent that we avoid committed relationships, to that extent our commitment remains only to one person—ourselves. And since our desires are often shaped by our mind, so commitment to ourselves essentially boils down to commitment to our mind, which frequently drags us down to self-defeating actions.

While any committed relationship can help us restrain our lower emotions, the higher emotions thus awakened aren't necessarily spiritual. Why? Because we may not be seeing ourselves or our loved ones spiritually—as souls, as spiritual parts of God. And without activating our spiritual side, we severely limit our access to higher emotions. Our highest, purest emotions come from our essential self—the soul. And the soul is the reservoir of pure emotions, for it is, as the Gita (15.07) states, a part of God, who is the supreme reservoir of pure emotions. As parts, we are meant to live in loving harmony with the Whole. Bhakti-yoga enables us to lovingly link with him and thereby activate our latent spiritual potential with its gamut of higher emotions.

There's another reason why, for bringing out our higher emotions, we need not just any committed relationship, but a committed relationship with God. Why? Because God alone is omnipotent. No matter how committed we may be to someone and no matter how good they may be, ultimately they don't have the power of God to purify and elevate us. Consider for example, the purifying potency of chanting the names of God. This potency is demonstrated in the Ramayana itself. Its composer, Valmiki, was a bandit who, by chanting the names of Rama, became a saint. Chanting the names of others can't bring about this kind of transformation—only God's names can.

A note of caution is warranted here. Bhakti is not about a relationship with God alone at the expense of our relationships with everyone else. The bhakti tradition reveals a vision of God who is not aloof from everyone, but is present in everyone and is the greatest benefactor of everyone. So, when our aspiration to love God is philosophically informed, we strive to love him by spiritually loving those whom he loves, which means everyone. We being finite can't practically express our love to everyone, but we can at least be sensitive and affectionate towards those with whom we relate regularly. Such an inclusive devotional vision can transmute our various relationships into crucibles for elevating our emotions.

To summarize, committing ourselves to a relationship with God elevates our emotions in three ways:

- Directing our emotion upwards as happens whenever we love someone.
- Uncovering the pure emotional power of the soul.
- Accessing the omnipotent grace of God.

Thus, while relationships in general can bring out the good within us, a relationship with God can bring out the best within us.

CHAPTER SIX

Rama-Bharata:
A Succession Conflict
Caused by Selflessness

When a wealthy patriarch dies, leaving behind a huge inheritance, frequently succession conflicts break out. While each conflict may have its specific dynamics, they all usually have a common denominator— selfishness. Everyone related with the deceased wants a share of the pie, with the progeny often wanting the biggest piece, if not the whole pie.

The Ramayana depicts a succession conflict between two princes after the death of their father. Strikingly however, this conflict is caused not by selfishness, but by selflessness. Rather than two brothers arguing to get the inheritance for themselves, they argue that the other should accept it. And no, the inheritance is not a white elephant—it is the flourishing kingdom of

Ayodhya, one of the most powerful kingdoms in ancient India. As intriguing as the conflict is, just as endearing is its resolution.

A Series of Shocks

When Bharata returns to Ayodhya, being summoned by the ministers, he is struck by a series of shocks—his father is dead; his brother is in exile; his mother is the cause of both these horrors; his mother has misunderstood him so much that she thinks he will be pleased by her machinations; many people, both courtiers and citizens, suspect him to be a co-conspirator with his mother. Steeling himself, he performs for his deceased father the elaborate funeral rites befitting a monarch, while resolving throughout to somehow set right at least some of the grievous wrongs. He decides to go personally to the forest for beseeching Rama to return and accept the throne.

Sincerity Removes Suspicion

When Bharata expresses his noble resolve to the courtiers, their lingering suspicions about his complicity are dissipated. His selflessness enlivens them, as does the possibility of their beloved Rama's return. They desire eagerly to accompany Bharata to the forest. He consents gladly, knowing that their presence will reinforce his request. The royal priest, Vashishtha, goes too, as does the chief minister, Sumantra, and the three recently widowed royal mothers—Kaushalya, Sumitra, and Kaikeyi. Understandably, Bharata has reservations about letting Kaikeyi accompany him. But she has had a change of heart, primarily because Bharata had reproached her and rejected her scheming. Seeing that she was sincerely repentant, he allows her to come, hoping that since she had asked for Rama's exile, maybe her request would influence him to end it too. When the citizens hear of Bharata's righteous resolve, they too are delighted, and many of them desire to go with him. Hoping that the gigantic show of strength will persuade Rama to return, Bharata orders that a road be constructed to take the huge procession into the forest.

Once the road is constructed, Bharata strives to retrace Rama's path, seeking the help of the tribal king, Guha, and the sage, Bharadwaja. Both of them initially express apprehension about Bharata's going to search for Rama with such a huge contingent. Their barely concealed suspicion about his intentions towards Rama shreds Bharata's heart. Controlling his pain, he expresses his fealty to his older brother with disarming sincerity, not only removing their suspicion but also winning their heart. They gladly show the way that Rama has taken.

Frequently, when people are accused of something, they feel angry, even when they are guilty, leave alone when they aren't. Bharata is repeatedly subjected to false accusations—and he has the royal power to silence his accusers. But far from angrily resorting to such power, he humbly wins over his accusers with his heart's power. By the sincere outpouring of his anguished heart, he fervently expresses his utter ignorance of, even revulsion with, the conspiracy against his brother and disarms those who had doubted him.

Love Wins—and So Does Duty

After a long journey through the dense forest and up the scenic mountain at Chitrakuta, Bharata broke into a clearing with a simple cottage. Seated outside the cottage were Rama, Sita, and Lakshmana. Bharata was anguished to see them all dressed in tree bark instead of the familiar royal robes. Falling at the feet of his eldest brother, Bharata spoke, "Alas! How cruel is fate that you, who are meant to live in royalty, are now living in poverty."

After greeting and consoling him, Rama enquired, "How is our venerable father? My heart is troubled on seeing the royal elephant, Shatrunjaya, riding in the procession without any ruler atop it." With a heavy heart, Bharata replied in a faltering voice, "Our glorious father, the illustrious king of Ayodhya, is no more."

Rama was grief-stricken, but somehow, he stoically pulled himself together and went to the nearby river for offering the oblation of water to his deceased father. His shock and grief subsided slowly, and his sense of royal responsibility came to the forefront. "Alas! Who will now occupy the throne? Who will protect Ayodhya from thieves and invaders?"

Seizing the moment as opportune, Bharata implored his brother to return, "The throne is meant for you, O brother. I can no more occupy the throne than can a crow take the position of an eagle."

Rama was gentle but firm in his refusal. "Now the only service I can render to our deceased father is to honour his memory by fulfilling his word. I will stay in the forest. You, O Bharata, should take the throne."

Bharata had already anticipated that Rama would not agree so easily. "Yes, O brother, our father's word must be honoured. Therefore, I will stay in the forest in your place—and you can return and become the king. Thus, our father's word will be honoured: one son of his will stay in the forest. And the kingdom will get a worthy king."

Seeing Bharata's astonishingly selfless offer, Rama smiled. "All of us have to bear our own karma; if people started interchanging their karma arbitrarily, the universal order will be thrown into chaos."

Their loving yet intense discussion went on for hours, with both brothers quoting scriptural and traditional precedents while trying to persuade each other to become the next king. The citizens were amazed and proud to see the brothers' erudition, which impressed and pleased even the assembled brahmins and sages. Despite their prolonged discussion, both remained unrelenting—Bharata in his request and Rama in his renunciation.

Seeing that Bharata wasn't making any headway, the elders came forward to try to persuade Rama. Vashishtha, the queens, Sumantra, and the accompanying brahmins, all gave various reasons why Rama should return. Rama heard their arguments and responded to them respectfully, without swerving from his position.

At this point, Bharata would have been justified in giving up. He could well have said that he hadn't caused Rama's exile and had done his best to get him back, perhaps thinking "If Rama isn't ready to listen, what can I do but accept the kingdom?" If a grand kingdom were providentially dropped into someone's lap, who wouldn't accept it? Bharata didn't.

Seeing his hopes of Rama's return dissipating, Bharata made a last-ditch plea. He sat on the forest floor declaring that he would sit there fasting till Rama accepted the kingdom. Everyone watched transfixed, waiting for Rama's response. After a momentous pause, Rama picked up Bharata, pulled him into an embrace, and told him, "O Bharata, your love has won." As Bharata's face blossomed with joy, Rama added with a sweet smile, "I accept the kingdom that you are offering me. But I also want to honour our father's word. So, after accepting the kingdom, I now entrust it to you for the fourteen-year exile period." Thus, Rama sagaciously resolved the dilemma, honouring both Bharata's love and his own duty.

Sandals as Symbols of Selflessness

Bharata was disappointed, but he knew that there's nothing more he could do to persuade Rama. Still, his selflessness found another endearing expression.

Often our ego makes us want to appear better than what we are—for example, people may use bombastic words to sound more learned than what they are or they may claim greater proximity with a famous person than their actual connection; or a caretaker-ruler may commandeer all the trappings of royalty to appear like the actual ruler. In contrast, Bharata wanted everyone to know his position—caretaker, not ruler. So, he requested Rama, "Please give me your sandals. I will place them on the throne and will sit on a seat below the throne." He thus ensured that the court's positions reflected his heart's disposition—Rama was the actual ruler and Bharata, his servitor.

After Rama obliged by offering his sandals, Bharata placed them on his head. Before departing, he made one final request, "Brother, please return as soon as fourteen years end. I won't be able to maintain my life for even one day beyond that—fourteen years of separation from you will be painful enough." Rama reassured that he would return, and Bharata left in tears.

On returning to Ayodhya, Bharata enthroned Rama's sandals. Sandals on a throne—such a symbol of selflessness will probably have few, if any, parallels in world history. In today's world, what brother would ask for another brother's sandals, except maybe to use them for smacking the other's head?

For the next fourteen years, Bharata shouldered all the responsibilities of the king, but refused all the privileges—quite the opposite of many present leaders who enjoy privileges without discharging responsibilities. Bharata lived in a hut outside the city at a place called Nandigram. Indeed, Bharata adopted a diet and dress similar to what Rama had adopted, thus performing in the kingdom the austerities Rama was performing in the forest.

A Test Passed with Delight

Bharata's selflessness was also evident at the end of the exile, in his eagerness to welcome Rama back. Rama knew that time has a dangerous power to erode even the noblest of intentions. So he wanted to check if, over the fourteen years, Bharata's emotions had changed, if he had become attached to the kingdom. If Bharata desired to stay on as its sovereign, Rama decided that he would not reclaim it. Accordingly, he called Hanuman and told him to go ahead of him to Ayodhya as a messenger and observer. "O Hanuman, inform Bharata that Rama will return soon, and observe whether he evinces any displeasure at this news." Ever eager to serve, Hanuman flew ahead, landed at Nandigram and conveyed Rama's message. The news filled Bharata with unrestrained jubilation. His face was a study in delight. He embraced and thanked Hanuman for bringing such great news, and offered him profuse thanks and abundant gifts. Bharata's facial and verbal expressions of joy left Hanuman in no doubt about the unreserved affection that the prince had for Rama.

Bharata rushed to arrange a majestic welcome for Rama. Soon, a huge congregation of courtiers and citizens assembled at the outskirts of Ayodhya, eagerly awaiting Rama's return. When they saw Rama with Sita, Lakshmana, and a large number of monkey warriors high in the sky aboard the celestial airplane Pushpaka, they gasped in astonishment and delight. As the plane descended, Bharata started offering articles of worship to the airborne Rama. After Rama disembarked, Bharata rushed forward and fell at the feet of his brother. Rama lovingly lifted and embraced him, their hearts joined together not just by proximity but also by the intensity that comes from the love that has withstood the toughest of tests.

Place Relations over Possessions

Valuing relations over possessions is foundational for the sustenance of family, society, and humanity at large. Bharata considered the affection that he relished in his relationship with Rama far more meaningful and fulfilling than the gratification of ruling the kingdom. Even if we can't be as selfless as him, still a slight increase in selflessness in our relationships can significantly improve them and substantially decrease conflicts.

The Ramayana's lessons run deeper than teaching us how to improve our relationships. Rama is not just a venerable elder brother—he is God himself descending to play the role of an ideal human being. Emotions directed towards him have the capacity to purify and elevate us, eventually granting us supreme liberation. The more we imbue our practice of bhakti-yoga with selflessness, the more our devotion becomes stronger, deeper, and sweeter, propelling us on the path to eternal spiritual fulfilment.

The evolution of selflessness thus progresses from valuing people over things to ultimately cherishing God over everything.

Selflessness Is Enriching, Not Impoverishing

A materialistic vision makes selflessness seem like self-deprivation. If matter and material things are the only source of enjoyment, then being selfless means depriving oneself of those things. Consequently, being selfless often equates living with less.

Though materialistic people may tout the word 'love' frequently, what actually goes on in the name of love is often an arrangement for mutual material gratification—when the gratification stops, the love too disappears. In contrast, a spiritual worldview helps us understand that our relationships are meant not for our material gratification, but for our spiritual evolution. That is, our relationships are meant to give us the realizations necessary for us to expand the scope of our love till it reaches the supreme spiritual reality—God. And loving him is not an isolated activity; he is, after all, the Lord of everyone, including our loved ones. So, the more we learn to love him, the more our love for our loved ones also becomes spiritualized and selfless, based not on the gratification they provide us, but on their connection with the One whom we aspire to love.

Moreover, the Lord is the source of all happiness, as is conveyed through the very name Rama; it means 'one who is the reservoir of all pleasure.' We can access this divine happiness by cultivating his loving remembrance. The greater our love, the more relishable becomes his remembrance. So, we start seeing love itself as life's supreme treasure—it is the greatest source of fulfilment, a fulfilment that becomes increasingly accessible through selflessness. Thus, we understand that selflessness is not impoverishing, but enriching.

Happiness Is the Byproduct, Not Product of Love

Someone may argue, "When we love the Lord because it makes us happy, then how is it actually selfless? Isn't it a form of selfishness too?"

Not necessarily. Initially we may strive to love the Lord with the hope of happiness. But even such less-than-selfless connection with the Lord purifies us, thus raising our love to a higher level. And for the highest, purest love, happiness is not the motive, but its natural result—happiness is not the product, but the byproduct. We don't love the Lord to be happy; we love him simply because he is so lovable. And by loving him purely, selflessly, wholeheartedly, we naturally relish the highest happiness. Pertinently, Srimad-Bhagavatam (1.2.6) states two significant characteristics of pure love for God as unmotivated and uninterrupted, conveying its selflessness; and as granting fulfilment to the heart, conveying its joyfulness. Thus, this sublime love is simultaneously selfless and joyful.

CHAPTER SEVEN

Sita-Lakshmana:
Intention in Tension?

'Stones and sticks may break my bones, but words will never hurt me.' This saying urges us to become thick-skinned and not let people's harsh words hurt us. It is an expression of a conscious intention, a rallying call to steel ourselves against painful words, whose power to injure is conveyed in another aphorism—'Words hurt more than swords.'

The Sinister Shapeshifter

The dynamics underlying these two paradoxical sayings can be understood from a pastime in the Ramayana. When Rama was living in the forest with his wife, Sita, and his younger brother, Lakshmana, they became the target of a conspiracy by the demon king Ravana who wanted to abduct Sita. He instructed one of his demon associates, a shapeshifting wizard named Maricha, to assume the form of a spellbindingly beautiful deer. It danced and pranced near Rama's forest cottage, captivating the tenderhearted Sita. She desired the deer as a pet to alleviate the austerity of forest life. Further, when their exile ended and they returned to Ayodhya, she could gift it as a memento to her mother-in-law, Kaushalya.

Pointing to the deer, Sita requested Rama to get it for her. Lakshmana, who was by Rama's side, peered at the deer. Where Sita saw disarming beauty, Lakshmana saw disconcerting peculiarity. Remarking that the deer looked too beautiful to be real, he pointed out that other animals were staying away from it. Given that deer are not predators, such fear for the deer among other animals was suspicious.

The Ramayana here points to an uncanny ability of animals to perceive things beyond human perception—an ability that some people living in, say, earthquake-prone areas sometimes testify to. Unusual behaviour such as fearfulness and noisiness among dogs, horses, and other similar animals often comprises a forewarning of an impending quake.

Based on the deer's unusual appearance and the other animals' uncharacteristic response to it, Lakshmana inferred that the deer was actually a demon. Sita, however, was so captivated that she neglected Lakshmana's inference and beseeched Rama again. Rama didn't have the heart to say no to her. She had given up so much for his sake in following him to the forest, and he, being bereft of all royal resources, had been able to give her so little in return. So, he decided to fulfil this small desire of hers by catching the deer.

On seeing Rama approaching, the deer took off into the forest. Rama gave chase and soon they both disappeared deep into the wilderness. Rama pursued the deer for nearly an hour. Whenever he closed in on it, it would escape by taking a giant leap, far bigger than what any deer would be capable of. Or it would just mystically disappear and reappear at a distance, as if teasing Rama. Tiring of its many tricks, Rama concluded that Lakshmana had been right—the deer was definitely a demon in disguise. Angered at its deception and wary of the danger it posed, he abandoned his plan to catch it alive and decided to kill it instead. Taking careful aim, he shot an arrow at the deer. Pierced mortally, the deer fell. The demon's shapeshifting abilities deserted him and he relapsed into his normal form as Maricha. Despite being fatally wounded, he summoned whatever residual abilities he had and imitated Rama's voice, calling to Lakshmana and Sita for help. His loud call resonated for several miles all around.

The Terrible Accusation

On hearing the call, Sita became overwhelmed by anxiety and agony. However, Lakshmana remained unperturbed and reassured Sita, "That voice is not Rama's. His archery prowess is supreme; no one can defeat him. I am sure that it is just a demon impersonating him."

But because the impersonation was so good, Sita didn't feel reassured by Lakshmana's words. Instead, she felt agitated by his actions or, more precisely, by his inaction. Fearing that Rama might be in danger—a danger that might degenerate to disaster if he was not helped—she urged and begged Lakshmana to go to Rama. On seeing her brother-in-law unmoved, she felt desperately driven to somehow trigger him into action. In a frenzy of anxiety, she accused him of having ill intentions towards her. "O Lakshmana, now I understand why you are not going to help Rama. You have an evil eye on me. You have come to the forest just to wait for an opportunity to act on your lusty desires. You think that if you don't go to help Rama, he will be slain, and then you can have your way with me." Shrieking in anxiety and anger, she said, "Never. I will die before you can touch me."

Sita's words cut Lakshmana deeper than had the sharpest arrows of the fiercest demons in the toughest of the battles he had fought. When he had always venerated Sita like his mother, to be accused of having lusty intentions towards her was horrifying. Further, he had the heart of a warrior who loved a good fight. Yet on Rama's instruction he had subordinated his martial instinct and accepted the role of a passive guard for Sita away from the scene of action while Rama played the role of the heroic warrior who bested demons. Despite having exhibited such dutiful subordination again and again, to be accused of doing nothing—and doing nothing so as to further his lusty desires—was excruciating. Most of all, Lakshmana loved his brother so much that he would have, without even a moment's hesitation, laid down his life for Rama's sake. To be accused that he was knowingly and intentionally staying passive while Rama was being killed was totally unbearable.

Lakshmana knew that Rama was in no danger and that Sita would be put in danger if he left her alone. Yet he could see no other way to stop her from hurling any more unbearable accusations at him, so he left her and went to search for Rama. Before departing, he drew a circle around the cottage, invested it with mystic protective power and requested Sita to stay within it. Then he departed, following his brother's trail deep into the forest.

Soon, he met Rama who was rushing back towards the cottage. On seeing Lakshmana, Rama immediately reproached him for having left Sita alone and unguarded. Lakshmana explained the words with which Sita had goaded him to leave. But Rama brushed them aside, telling Lakshmana that he shouldn't have taken her sentimental words spoken in anxiety so seriously. Put another way, Rama essentially stated—don't ascribe ill intention to what is spoken in tension.

Rama's words helped Lakshmana calm down. They both realized that a conspiracy was afoot. The demon's taking on a deer form to captivate Sita, its evasive flight into the forest to take Rama far away from Sita, and its final cry in the voice of Rama to get Lakshmana away from Sita—all these were parts of a scheme to make Sita alone and defenseless in the cottage. Her harsh words to Lakshmana had unwittingly furthered the conspiracy, as had Lakshmana's reaction to those words. Realizing the great danger Sita would be in, they both rushed back to the cottage. But it was too late; she had already been abducted.

The Battle between the Head and the Tongue

Sita and Lakshmana are transcendental, being intimate associates of Rama—by their actions, they assist him in his pastimes according to his divine plan. So, rather than judging whether Sita was wrong in speaking those hurtful words or whether Lakshmana was wrong in taking those words too seriously, we can focus instead on how we can choose our words and our responses to others' words carefully.

In the backdrop of this pastime, let's revisit the two starting sayings about the power of words. The saying 'words can never hurt me' can be seen as an exhortation to the injured party to not take hurting words too seriously. The saying 'words hurt more than swords' can be seen as an exhortation to a potential injurer to check oneself before verbally lashing out at others. At different times amidst life's vicissitudes, we may be either the injured or the injurer. So, depending on context, both these sayings can guide us.

Life's unpalatable reality is that, no matter how nice we are to people, they will sometimes speak hurting words. When such words come from our loved ones, they often hurt much more than when they come from our antagonists. Pain is often a function of expectation and preparation. When we expect a punch, we steel ourselves against it—the punch still hurts, but the hurt is decreased by our preparedness. However, when we expect a pat and receive a punch instead, the punch catches us unawares and hurts us more. Similarly, when we are with our antagonists, we expect harsh words and steel ourselves against them. But when we are with our loved ones, we expect kind words. When we receive harsh words instead, those words sting intolerably, as happened with Lakshmana on hearing Sita's accusatory words.

In our relationships, how can we prevent passing words from causing lasting ruptures? By meditating that words spoken in tension seldom reflect intention. Tension often makes our head lose the battle with our tongue. And we end up speaking hurting words without really meaning what we are saying. Just as we are prone to this human weakness, so are others. Just as we would want others to excuse us for such lapses, we too should excuse others' similar lapses.

Don't See Through Others; See Others Through

A question may surface: "Even if someone speaks when in tension, should absolutely no intention be ascribed to their words? No matter how stressed they might have been, doesn't the very fact that they spoke certain things suggest that they must have thought something in that direction earlier? After all, if there is smoke, shouldn't there be some fire somewhere?"

A more pertinent question is: Should we be judging others based on the contents of the smokiest chambers of their heart? Would we want others to judge us by that standard?

We all are contaminated by many past negative impressions, and we live in a culture that further contaminates us. So, dark thoughts may surface within us even against our intentions. Bhagavad-gita (03.36) mentions that there exists within our psyche something that impels us forcefully towards actions that are against our intentions. If we were to be judge and condemn others for the dark thoughts that might pass through their minds—thoughts that occasionally come out as words—then we would probably have to condemn ourselves first. So, if someone who is usually kind-hearted suddenly speaks something harsh, we needn't let that one outburst overshadow their past track record. Why let a potentially lasting relationship become hostage to one verbal lapse?

By the arrangement of nature and ultimately of God, we can see only the expressions and actions of others, not their thoughts. This barrier in perception serves as an essential protector of all relationships. If everyone could see everything that passed through everyone's minds, everyone would be shocked by the unworthy thoughts that incidentally pass through others' minds, thereby making any relationship almost impossible to sustain. The barrier between our thoughts on one hand and our words and actions on the other hand provides us room for self-regulation—for restraining our lower side, and expressing our higher side. Thus, we can attain self-mastery and gradually bring out the best within us.

If we are on the verge of speaking without thinking, we can create a pause button for ourselves by, say, counting till ten or, better still, chanting the holy names of God ten times. If anger keeps choking us internally, we can vent it out in a journal, thus getting it out of our system without scorching others, as it would if spoken directly to them. Getting the anger out of our system will calm us down. Then we can revisit what we have written and use our intelligence to evaluate whether our anger is justified. If it is, we can determine the most appropriate way of expressing it so that we can help in clarifying any misconception and rectifying any misdemeanour.

We are not here to see through each other; we are here to see each other through. Keeping this cooperative focus in mind can make our relationships symbiotic, not antagonistic.

The Divine Centre for Relationships

A symbiotic vision of relationships based on mutual cooperation is easier to sustain when we study scripture and internalize a spiritual vision of life. When we understand that we are eternal spiritual beings on a multi-life journey towards God, we see others as co-pilgrims on this journey. We will be together for a brief lifetime, and we don't know what our destination will be thereafter. From this long-term perspective, we can see others' occasional harsh words as accidental—something like an unintentional elbow jab while travelling in a crowded train.

No doubt, harsh words from loved ones cut far deeper than does an elbow jab. And overlooking those words is much more difficult because the doubt lingers that some ill intention might have been lurking somewhere in their heart. When we have been badly hurt, we may need to convey in some appropriate way the magnitude of the wound and the gravity of the wounding words. Further, the healing of our emotions and the restoration of our trust may need time—time during which the hurting party demonstrates the absence of any ill-intention through consistent actions. Depending on the situation, the specific measures we take to help heal the relationship may vary. But underlying these varying specifics is the common denominator of the willingness to let go of the past.

By holding on to something that someone might have unintentionally spoken during a tense situation, we poison our consciousness and paralyze our capacity for loving interactions. By choosing instead to focus on the good side of our loved ones and overlooking any uncharacteristic lapse, we can preserve the steady relationship that can help bring out our higher side and their higher side too.

Further, by practising bhakti-yoga regularly, we can bring God into the centre of our lives and our relationships. Then we can see others as connected with God and see all interactions as opportunities to grow in spiritual devotion. What if we want a God-centred relationship, but the other party doesn't want to be God-centred or doesn't act in a godly way? Still, if we centre our heart on God by taking fervent shelter of him, we can get the solace and strength necessary to endure any disappointment in that relationship. Then we will understand that we are acting in that relationship not so much to serve them as to serve God through them—so our behaviour with them should be determined not just by how they behave but by how God would want us to behave in that situation. Such a meditation can empower us to respond to insensitivity with maturity.

Acting with this vision, we can not only improve our relationships with others but can also increasingly relish our supremely fulfilling relationship with God. By focusing on him and on how we can best serve him, we can choose words and actions that are growth-inducing.

Sita and Lakshmana, despite their heart-wrenching interaction before her abduction, were centred on the service of Rama. And by keeping his service at the centre of their lives, they were able to put aside this terrible interaction and move on in their relationship. Sita and Lakshmana met again after Rama won the climactic war against Ravana's vicious hordes. Neither Sita nor Lakshmana mentioned their traumatic parting. Even before that, neither of them blamed the other for what had happened. Lakshmana recognized that what Sita had spoken was out of trepidation, not suspicion—and he let her words pass. So can we.

CHAPTER EIGHT

Maricha-Rama:
To Die at Someone's Hands
or for Someone's Hands?

We all are going to die one day. This is one of life's hardest truths—hard to endure and hard even to contemplate. Equipping us to face this reality, Gita wisdom explains that we are at our core eternal souls; death is an event that happens only to our bodies, not to our souls.

Seen in this light, death is not a termination but a transition. Where do we go after death? That is determined by how we live and how we leave. Our post-mortem destination is determined by the consciousness we have at the time of death, which in turn is determined by the consciousness we cultivate throughout our life. (Bhagavad-gita 08.06-07). If we die remembering God, we attain him (Gita 08.05).

The Ramayana depicts a fascinating character Maricha who uses this knowledge about one's post-mortem destination to make a decision that is life-defining, or, to put it more fittingly, life-ending. But whether his decision is right or not is open to debate—a debate that reveals the difference between self-centredness and God-centredness in the application of spiritual knowledge.

Self-actualizing Fear

Maricha appeared first in the 'Bala-kanda,' the first book of the Ramayana, wherein Rama was still young and unmarried. The Ayodhya prince had gone to the forest with the sage, Vishwamitra, to protect the sage's sacrifices from being desecrated by demons. When Maricha along with the demoness Tataka and her son Subahu attacked Vishwamitra's sacrifice, Rama along with Lakshmana countered them. Rama slew Tataka and Subhahu, but Maricha was spared, being hit by a blunt arrow shot by Rama. Though blunt, that arrow was so forceful that it hurled him a long distance away. A demon powerful enough to hurl trees far away with the force of his arms found himself hurled far away by the force of Rama's arrows.

The trauma of that forced flight left Rama's awesome power forever impressed in Maricha's mind. Having experienced Rama's incomparable and unbearable power, he had a change of heart induced by fear. Recognizing that he would never be able to counter Rama, he decided to give up his demoniac way of life and atone for his past misdeeds by becoming an austere sage. He lived on simple forest fare, chanted mantras, and meditated on higher spiritual reality, yet he lived in constant fear of Rama. Such was his fear that even hearing the syllable 'Ra' petrified him, for he dreaded that the sound of that syllable would be followed by the bow-wielding Rama, who would kill him. Maricha understood that Rama was God descended in human form in this world, but he didn't understand that God is benevolent, not malevolent.

Whatever we fear fervently, we may draw towards ourselves by that concentrated negative mental energy. Our fears can become like our self-actualizing and self-sabotaging prophecies. Of course, our thinking about a thing doesn't alone make that thing happen. But our obsessive thinking can make us do the actions that can set up the circumstances which induce that thing to happen. Maricha who lived constantly in fear of Rama's arrows eventually died of those arrows, despite performing austerities to avoid that fate.

Constrained into Conspiracy

To understand how this happens, we pick up the Ramayana storyline at the point when the demon-king Ravana was scheming to abduct Rama's consort, Sita. Having heard of Rama's formidable prowess, Ravana decided to avoid a head-on confrontation with Rama. He hatched a conspiracy for sidelining Rama and conscripted Maricha into that conspiracy.

Maricha was a specialist at shape-changing. Many demons had shape-shifting abilities but Maricha's shape shifting abilities were extraordinary even among demons. Knowing this, Ravana went to Maricha and told him about the scheme. Maricha's normal fear of Rama heightened to terror when he heard about Ravana's plan to abduct Rama's wife.

Vehemently and desperately, he begged Ravana, "O king of demons, please don't provoke Rama. That Ayodhya prince's power is unmatchable. To anger him is to court death." Not wanting to appear as if he was criticizing Ravana for entertaining the idea of abducting Sita, he changed tack and asked, "What enemy of yours has planted this horrible idea in your head? That person deserves to be punished." Feeling cautioned by Maricha's assessment of Rama's power, Ravana reluctantly abandoned his plan to abduct Sita.

At this point, Ravana had wanted to abduct Sita primarily because he saw her as a means by which he could get back at Rama for having destroyed the demons whom he had stationed at his outpost at Janasthana. Women are often treated as pawns in the power games of men, but then, women too treat men as pawns in their power games. Little did Ravana know that he was soon going to become such a pawn in the hands of his sister, Shurpanakha.

This demoness felt that she has been dishonoured by Rama, and wanted Ravana to punish him. When Ravana remained reluctant, she incited him by describing Sita's devastating beauty, and the lusty demon's intelligence soon lay devastated. Ravana resolved to abduct Sita and again went to Maricha and ordered him to assist.

When Maricha started to protest, Ravana silenced him with an ultimatum: "Do as I say or I will kill you." Resorting to his royal haughtiness, Ravana declared, "I have come to you to give instruction, not to take suggestion." Maricha realized that the demon king was beyond listening to any good counsel and reluctantly decided to go along with Ravana's scheme. He reasoned that his death was inevitable—so he might as well choose the best death, that is, the death that would lead to the best possible destination in his afterlife. Dying at the hands of Rama would lead to his elevation, possibly even liberation, whereas dying at the hands of Ravana would take him to some unknown destination.

Resigning himself to fate, he assumed the form of an irresistibly attractive deer. He started playing near Rama's hermitage, thereby attracting Sita's attention. Soon, she begged Rama to get the deer as a pet for her. Rama moved to catch the deer, but it flew away, and Rama followed. The deer kept bounding away, suddenly jumping a huge distance, suddenly disappearing and reappearing at a distance, and doing things impossible for ordinary deer. Rama's suspicion about the identity of the deer increased, and finally when the deer led him far into the forest, he decided to shoot it. On being struck by Rama's arrow, the deer called out loudly in the voice of Rama, "O Lakshmana,

O Sita, help!" Hearing it, Rama realized that the deer's drawing him away from Sita was a plot by the demons to catch her unguarded. Alarmed, he veered around to rush back to his hermitage.

As Rama turned around, Maricha breathed his last. While dying, he beheld Rama. He achieved his purpose of dying in Rama's presence, but he died while working against Rama's purpose.

Self-centred or God-centred?

The great bhakti saint, Bhaktivinod Thakura, states in his book *Chaitanya Shikshamrita* that people may approach God at different levels—fear, desire, duty, and love. When we approach God out of fear or even out of desire, we are largely self-centred since we are thinking, "What can God do for me?" Connecting with God at any level may be better than a godless life, still a devotional connection is centred on the object of our love—we approach God to serve him for his pleasure.

At one level, Maricha's reasoning that dying at Rama's hands was better than dying at Ravana's hands reflects his spiritual knowledge. He had the knowledge that he will continue to exist after death and that his post-mortem destination would be positively impacted by dying in Rama's presence.

At another level, however, his failure to consider whether he was working for Rama's purpose or against it reflects that he hasn't internalized the purpose of spiritual knowledge—to rise from self-centredness to God-centredness. Despite his spiritual knowledge, he didn't think of Rama and Rama's service; he thought only of his own elevation and destination. Because of his self-centredness, he perceived God as a tool for his elevation, not as the purpose of his elevation. Bhakti wisdom explains that we are God's eternal parts, and when we harmonize with him by learning to love him selflessly, we find life's highest satisfaction. We become absorbed in the Lord's loving service, an absorption that eventually elevates us to his eternal abode for a life of immortal love with him.

In jarring contrast to such selfless service, Maricha ended up working against the person whom he should have been serving.

Could he have done anything differently? Wasn't he left with no choice when Ravana threatened him with death if he refused to cooperate? Yes, his choices were constricted, but still he could have used his intelligence. Maybe he could have gotten away from Ravana by nominally agreeing to go along with the demon's scheme, but could then have taken shelter of Rama. He could have alerted Rama to the conspiracy that was afoot and have thus helped foil the abduction of Sita. Rama would surely have protected him, just as he protected another demon who sought his shelter. Later in the Ramayana, just before the final war between Rama and Ravana, Vibhishana, a younger brother of Ravana, came over to Rama's side, being appalled by Ravana's unrepentant viciousness.

Though Vibhishana was not explicitly threatened with death by Ravana, he knew well what that demon-king would do to those whom he considered traitors—kill in the most heartless and cruelest possible way. Despite the risks, Vibhishana followed his intelligence and conscience. In contrast, Maricha simply obeyed Ravana in his fiendish scheme to abduct a virtuous lady.

At yet another level, the various characters in the Lord's pastimes can be seen transcendentally—they are furthering his pastimes by acting as needed, sometimes acting congenially and sometimes inimically. Nonetheless, if we wish to learn ethical lessons from those pastimes and thereby make wiser decisions in our own lives, we can learn a valuable lesson from Maricha. He serves as an excellent example of a person whose knowledge is nullified by his lack of understanding of the purpose of that knowledge. Thus, he antagonizes the person who is the purpose of that knowledge.

Models of Devotion—and of Non-devotion

Another bhakti saint, Rupa Goswami, offers a relevant insight in his classic devotional guidebook, *The Bhakti Rasamrita Sindhu*. He states that only those activities that are performed with a favourable disposition towards the Lord, seeking to please him, are considered devotional activities. When the Lord's service is not the intention, then what is performed is not devotion, even if it is performed in relationship with him. Though such action may lead to some elevation in one's post-mortem destination, devotees don't seek such an elevation that is divorced from devotion. That's why Maricha is never considered a model of devotion, whereas Vibhishana is.

When we practice bhakti, our focus is not so much on how we die but how we live—not at whose hands we die, but for whose hands we live and, if necessary, die. For whose hands we live and die means for whose purpose we dedicate our life. Srimad-Bhagavatam states that the Lord executes his will sometimes through his own hands and sometimes through the hands of his devotees, those who work for him. The process of bhakti-yoga helps us become the Lord's hands. When we become devoted, we think not so much of our pleasure in this life or even our destination after this life, we think primarily about our Lord's purpose and his service. To live for him and to die for him is the purpose and perfection of devotion.

Another character with whom Maricha can be contrasted is Jatayu, who died just a few hours after Maricha. Jatayu was an aged vulture who attained martyrdom while trying to stop Ravana from abducting Sita. Rama felt deeply indebted to Jatayu for his death-embracing service. Rama personally performed the last rites for Jatayu, just as a son would perform for his father. Though Jatayu was killed at the hands of a demon, he died for the hands of the Lord, working for his purpose. In fact, he died in the hands of the Lord, breathing his last with his head resting on Rama's lap and his eyes beholding Rama's divine face.

With such a supremely auspicious departure, he attained the supreme destination in his afterlife.

In whose presence we die is not as important as for whose purpose we die—and for whose purpose we live. How to live in devotion, risking death for the Lord's sake, is exemplified by Vibhishana. And how to leave in devotion, embracing death for the Lord's sake, is exemplified by Jatayu. Unfortunately, Maricha's misguided choice means that he exemplifies neither.

CHAPTER NINE

Rama-Shabari:
The Intent of a Gift Matters
More Than Its Content

Don't look a gift horse in the mouth. This saying originates from the traditional practice of determining a horse's age and thereby its value by looking at its teeth. The saying implies that we shouldn't be ungrateful for a gift or find faults with it. One way we might fault a gift is by evaluating it solely in monetary terms and minimizing it if it isn't expensive enough.

Such restraint is necessary because of not just courtesy but also sensitivity. Different people express their affection by giving gifts in terms that they value. If we don't understand the value of what they value, we may neglect or even reject their gift.

Suppose someone offers us an art masterpiece that is worth millions. If we don't have an eye for art, we may think of it as just a good-looking painting and put it aside. But an expert would tell us the gift's value.

Even in this example, the value, though not discernible to the untrained eye, is still measurable financially. But what if the value transcends the financial dimension? What if it expresses the heart's deep affection that is beyond monetary valuation? To appreciate such gifts, we need to expand our conceptions of valuation.

A Fishy Gift

The Ramayana describes two incidents that depict Rama's sensitivity when offered gifts that would normally not have been valued as much had it been some other ruler of his position in an illustrious ruling dynasty.

The first incident occurred soon after Rama was exiled. While he was on his way to the forest, a devout fisherman offered him some fish. Rama being a scion in the cultured Raghu family didn't partake meat. Yet he didn't brush off the offering. Why? Because though he had no taste for fish, he could taste the love of the giver of the fish.

Some people, even some professedly pious people, see interactions as a way of scoring brownie points in a morality contest. Whenever they see someone doing something that they consider wrong, they become derisive or dismissive towards them. By such conduct, they not only alienate others materially, but also impede others' spiritual growth and their own spiritual growth too.

By accepting that none of us are ever morally perfect—we all have our follies and foibles, struggles and secrets—we can avoid the judgmentality that leads to insensitivity.

Contaminated Berry, Pure Heart

Later, when Rama was searching for Sita who had been abducted by the demon king, Ravana, he came to the hermitage of Matanga *rishi*. There, he met the sage's female ascetic disciple, Shabari. She had been waiting for many years to serve Rama. When her guru had departed from this world, he had taken most of his disciples with him. But he had asked Shabari to stay on, assuring her that she was meant to do a special service to the Lord when he would descend to this world. Now, when she beheld Rama coming to her abode through the forest, she realized that her dream had come true.

She had dreamt that whenever Rama would appear, she would offer him the best berries growing in the nearby forest. But she faced a practical problem—How was she to know which berries were good and which weren't? By looking at them, especially their colour, she could infer which were raw and which ripe. But she couldn't accurately infer how sweet they were. Having no taster other than herself readily at hand, she had made a practice of tasting the berries herself. She would take a small bite from the corner of a berry. However, given the berry's small size, a small bite would amount to a significant portion of the berry. On tasting that bite, she would cast aside the berries that were not sweet enough and preserve carefully the sweet ones. She had followed this routine, day after day, month after month, year after year, longing for the day when the Lord of her heart would appear before her eyes.

And now, that momentous day had come. When Rama came before her, her joy knew no bounds. Offering Rama and his brother, Lakshmana, a seat, she proceeded to offer them the best of her berries. To parse the berries, she followed her standard procedure of biting them and then offered the sweet ones to Rama and Lakshmana.

Lakshmana was taken aback. In orthodox brahminical societies, food touched by someone else's mouth is considered contaminated. The only exception to this rule were spiritually exalted souls, whose remnants were considered sanctified, and the opportunity to take that food was considered a special blessing. Shabari belonged to a tribal community that was by no means considered high-class; so, the food touched by her mouth would be conventionally deemed contaminated.

Rama too saw what Lakshmana saw, but he saw more. He saw beyond the contaminated berry to the pure heart that was offering it. Appreciating Shabari's pure intention to offer him the best berries, he accepted and ate them. He savoured not just the berries' sweetness but also Shabari's devotion.

This action of Rama was radical, when considered in

the light of the prevailing emphasis on ritual purity. If a person in an exalted social position ate food cooked by people with contaminated consciousness, such eating was considered a serious lapse in that person's purity. Travelling mendicants would sometimes prefer to stay hungry than eat contaminated food. Today, we may find such standards extreme, but we can appreciate them better if we see beyond the specific practices to their essential purpose. That purpose was to protect from contamination the consciousness of those who had centred their life on purifying their consciousness.

Rama demonstrates that we shouldn't let considerations of ritual purity come in the way of our loving reciprocations, especially when those reciprocations can help people rise to higher consciousness from wherever they are presently.

The Many Languages of Love

Whenever people offer us something, they are, in their own way, offering us their affection. Through their language, they are opening a door to their heart. Depending on how we reciprocate with their invitation, they will decide whether to further open the door of their heart or shut it.

Language here doesn't refer to the verbal tool for communication but to the psychological disposition that shapes how we look at things, what we see in the world, and how we make sense of what we see. Even if two people are speaking the same verbal language, they may be speaking in very different languages if they have different orientations, say, if one of them is more emotional than rational and the other, more rational than emotional.

This understanding of different conceptual languages is seconded by modern psychology. Books about the different psychological natures of men and women, or about different personality types, stress that we can't truly understand others unless we get their language.

When we stretch ourselves, that is, expand our conceptual frameworks to learn others' language, a whole new world will open in our relationships with them—we will get to know them much better.

Spirituality More Important Than Morality and Purity

Such expansion of our conceptual frameworks is essential for appreciating spirituality, especially devotional spirituality. When we approach God, he sees the language our heart is speaking. In one of the most endearing verses of the Bhagavad-gita (09.26), he declares that he accepts a fruit, a flower, a leaf, or even a little water if it is offered with devotion. The Lord who is fully self-satisfied becomes hungry for our offering when we infuse it with devotional intent. Indeed, devotion is his appetizer. No matter how materially insignificant our offering may be, he accepts it and reciprocates by giving us his mercy. That mercy further opens our heart towards loving him and progressing towards him.

Undoubtedly, to practise bhakti seriously, we need to follow certain standards of morality and purity. Morality and purity are routes for offering and receiving love. When we love someone, we are at our best around that person—that is the nature of love, it brings out the best within us. And love for the supreme person, the Lord, who is the abode of all morality and purity, brings out our best side. Devotion empowers us to rise from our present level to higher standards of morality and purity. Complementarily, Rama, as the Lord of everything including morality and purity, is pleased when we make our offerings while striving to live according to high moral and ritual standards. And yet when someone offers him something with genuine devotion, he doesn't let the absence of standards interfere with the reciprocation of love.

When dealing with others, especially those who are not devotional practitioners, we need to follow the Lord's example of focusing on essential intention. If we let judgmentality about morality and purity block the flow of positive intention, we cut off the greatest propeller for their self-transformation—the sweetness of divine loving reciprocations. It is primarily such reciprocations that will inspire them to purify and elevate themselves.

When we follow in our Lord's footsteps and focus on the essence of reciprocating love, we will find that the opportunities to have fulfilling exchanges with others will multiply manifold. We will see many situations that we had earlier dismissed as morally unfavourable and impure as being nonetheless rich in spiritual potential.

In general, by learning to focus on the essence, beyond externals, we can go deeper into the substance of devotion to the Lord who pervades all of reality. We will relish deeper, stronger, sweeter devotion and become centred on him, thus realizing our heart's deepest desire to love and be loved, eternally.

CHAPTER TEN

Jatayu-Ravana:
Victorious in Defeat

No one likes to lose. When we find ourselves losing, we often try to connect with someone stronger to emerge victorious. When people start worshiping God, they frequently do so in the hope that he will help them win their battles. Indeed, the world's scriptures contain celebrated narratives of how the devoted overcame herculean odds by divine grace.

Still, scriptures also contain alternative narratives wherein the devoted are defeated. How are such narratives to be understood? By expanding our conceptions beyond the material to the spiritual.

Such narratives compel us to recognize how our own existence and God's protection extend beyond the material level of reality. If we expect that God will ensure our worldly success each and every time, then our faith will be shaken, even shattered, by worldly reversals. More importantly, we will deprive ourselves of the many eternal blessings available at the spiritual level of reality.

Doomed yet Determined

To understand how spiritual vision can change our perception of reversals, let's look at the Ramayana story of the vulture, Jatayu. He is best known for having attained martyrdom while trying to stop Ravana from abducting Sita. That lecherous demon had conspired to abduct Sita by sidetracking her protectors. As he was carrying Sita through the airways in his mystic chariot, Sita desperately called for help. Though Rama and Lakshmana couldn't hear, being too far away, someone else heard and acted.

Sita saw the vulture Jatayu rising from a tree. This elderly bird had been a friend of Dasharatha, Sita's late father-in-law, and was residing in the Dandaka forest. When Rama, Sita, and Lakshmana had come to that forest, Jatayu had welcomed them with paternal affection. He had assured Rama that he would help protect Sita in the dangerous, demon-infested forest. True to his word, Jatayu was now flying to her rescue.

Being the wife of a warrior, Sita quickly assessed the comparative strengths of Ravana and Jatayu. She realized that the aged bird would be no match for the younger and stronger demon. So, she called out to him, "Please just inform Rama that Ravana has abducted me. Don't try to stop Ravana, for this demon will kill you."

But Jatayu found heeding Sita's warning impossible. How could he live with himself if he did nothing to stop her abduction? Despite knowing that he would be hard-pressed to match Ravana, he felt driven to protect her by doing everything within his power. Determinedly, he flew by the side of Ravana, rebuking his irreligiosity in abducting a married woman. As expected, that discourse on virtue didn't deter the vile demon. Jatayu promptly changed tack and challenged him to a fight. When the demon kept flying on, Jatayu goaded him by calling him a coward who had kidnapped Sita behind Rama's back. When Ravana still didn't respond, Jatayu resorted to the only option left for him—attack.

He pierced Ravana's arms with his talons, caught his hair in his beaks, and pulled him around. Ravana roared in fury, feeling humiliated at being dragged thus by a mere vulture—that too in front of the woman he wanted to impress and have as his new chief-queen. Initially, he had neglected the vulture, thinking him to be a powerless interferer. But when Jatayu attacked him so fiercely, he decided to fight and kill him.

Ravana soon found that Jatayu, far from being an easy prey, was a seasoned fighter. Jatayu's plan was to first immobilize the demon, then attack and kill him. If Ravana managed to fly off in his chariot, Jatayu would have no chance of saving Sita. Accordingly, he forcefully targeted and finished the mules moving Ravana's chariot. With just one hit of his bill, he felled the charioteer. Then, with repeated blows, he shattered the chariot.

Meanwhile, Ravana had been counter-attacking Jatayu with arrows discharged from his gigantic bow. But the bird had shrugged off the arrows and continued his attack. As his chariot fell to pieces, Ravana was forced to descend to the ground, holding Sita in one hand and his bow in the other. From the ground, the infuriated demon showered so many arrows on Jatayu that they covered him like a nest covering a bird. Though wounded, Jatayu kept attacking Ravana, eventually breaking his bowstring. But Ravana quickly strung another bow and counter-attacked.

Evading some arrows and enduring others, Jatayu swooped down on Ravana. With astonishing strength, he ripped off one of the demon's arms. But to his consternation, that arm grew back right away. Ravana had received a benediction from Brahma that whenever his limbs would be cut, they would grow back. Though Jatayu dismembered Ravana repeatedly, the cut limbs grew back within moments.

Over time, Jatayu grew tired and his movements became slower. Soon, Ravana, while parrying the bird's attack, sensed his opportunity. As the bird flew away from him, Ravana moved with lightning speed, using his sword to lop off one wing. In no time, he had lopped off the other wing too. Bleeding profusely, Jatayu fell to the ground. Crying in dismay, Sita, who had shrunk away from the gruesome fight, ran towards Jatayu to comfort him. With a victorious roar, Ravana dragged her by her hair. By his mystic power, he rose into the sky and flew away, leaving Jatayu writhing in helpless agony.

The Last Service with the Last Breath

Though mortally wounded, Jatayu grittily maintained his life. He remembered that Sita had requested him to inform Rama about her abduction. He had tried to do more, but had failed. Nonetheless, he was determined to fulfil Sita's request. Despite being in severe pain, he waited, calling out the name of Rama and finding solace in that sacred chant.

Meanwhile, Rama, along with Lakshmana, was frantically searching for Sita. In due course of time, he came to a forest clearing that had evidently been the arena of a brutal battle. With upraised bow, he looked around grimly, dreading that Sita might have met her end here. Noticing a creature lying on the ground nearby, Rama thought that it was Sita's demoniac abductor in bird form and prepared to shoot it with his bow. Jatayu was so badly mutilated that Rama couldn't recognize him.

What a test of faith it must have been for Jatayu when he saw Rama's arrow pointed at him—the very same person for whom he had risked his life was about to take his life! Yet he faithfully continued chanting Rama's name, his voice faint due to his diminishing strength. But Rama heard that faint chant. Intrigued, he lowered his bow and observed carefully. When he recognized the bird to be Jatayu, he ran forward and embraced him. With his last few breaths, Jatayu explained what had happened. Having performed his final service of informing Rama about Sita's abduction, he fell silent forever.

Grief-struck, Rama personally performed the last rites for Jatayu—an unprecedented act of divine grace that trumped social convention and guaranteed Jatayu life's supreme success.

Auspiciousness amidst Inauspiciousness

Spiritual wisdom helps us understand that we are indestructible souls on a multi-life transmigratory journey towards eternal liberation, a life of spiritual love with God. We are all fighting a war against worldly illusions that allure us with temporary pleasures and deprive us of everlasting happiness.

In this war, more important than succeeding in avoiding death—an avoidance that can't anyway be continued forever—is succeeding in remembering God, the highest reality beyond the world of death. The Bhagavad-gita (08.05-06) explains that our mentality at death determines our post-mortem destiny. If our consciousness is fixed on God at the time of death, we attain his eternal abode. Therefore, remembering God at death is life's crowning success. This success gives a reward far greater than the reward from many victories in life's various battles, which will anyway be undone with the final defeat at death. Though Jatayu lost his battle with Ravana, he achieved the supremely rewarding success by dying in Rama's presence, absorbed in his remembrance.

And that he achieved such sterling success while being in a vulture body is all the more remarkable. In the Vedic tradition, vultures often symbolize ignorance, for they feast on corpses, which are considered extremely impure.

But Jatayu, despite being in such a vulture-body, achieved the supreme fortune of dying in the presence of the Lord. In the bhakti tradition, the grandsire of the Kuru dynasty, Bhishma, is celebrated for having achieved the ideal death because Krishna was right next to him during his final moments. Long before Bhishma, Jatayu too achieved a similar ideal departure by leaving his mortal shell not just in the Lord's presence, but also on his lap.

And Jatayu's fortune didn't end there. After he departed, Rama, performing his last rites, offered him the same honour that a son offers his father.

Losing the Battle, Winning the War

War strategists know that accepting defeat in a small battle to win a big battle is no loss. Spiritual vision helps us see defeat at the physical level to be like losing one battle in a war. But if that defeat impels us to increase our remembrance of God, then that increased remembrance is a significant spiritual gain. And if it inspires us to remember him at the time of death, then losing the battle of survival in this life to win the war for attaining eternal peace in the afterlife is a winning gambit.

Of course, it's unlikely that we will be asked to make such extreme sacrifices, but whatever challenges we need to face or losses we need to sustain in our service to the Lord, we can be assured that we will ultimately be the supreme gainers.

However, if victories at the physical level make us believe that we can be successful and happy in this world, and that we don't need to raise our consciousness to the spiritual level, then worldly illusion has scored a major victory over us, for we are now proudly situated in its clutches. Though we may have won the battle in this world, we have sustained one more defeat in our multi-life war against illusion.

In contrast, Jatayu lost the battle against Ravana, but he won the war against worldly illusion. He was victorious in defeat. Bhakti wisdom invites all of us to similarly win life's ultimate war.

CHAPTER ELEVEN

Vali-Sugriva:
Judging without Understanding

Apoignant subplot in the Ramayana is the fratricidal confrontation between the two monkey brothers, Vali and Sugriva. In the Mahabharata, fraternal animosity between the virtuous Pandavas and the evil Kauravas continues till the death of the Kauravas. In contrast, the Ramayana features deathbed reconciliation between the simian siblings that is as emotionally riveting as it is ethically illuminating.

The Awesome Twosome

The story of these two brothers unfolded in Kishkinda, the kingdom of the *Vanaras* (monkeys) in southern India. The Vanaras were a race of celestial monkeys possessing formidable strength and intelligence, with some monkey-leaders having more sapient attributes than simian. Kishkinda's location was geopolitically significant, being situated strategically between the kingdom of humans in the north and the kingdom of demons in the south. Throughout their childhood and youth, Vali and Sugriva were inseparable. Like the Pandavas, they both had dual sires—one earthly, one heavenly. Their earthly father was Riksharaja, the king of the Vanaras. And their heavenly fathers were Indra and Surya respectively, two of the most powerful gods. Just as Indra was higher in the cosmic hierarchy than Surya, Vali, being older and stronger, was higher than Sugriva. Just as Indra was given to bouts of arrogance and impetuosity, so was Vali. Just as the two gods worked harmoniously in the cosmic administration, their two sons worked harmoniously in the administration of the monkey kingdom. When Riksharaja retired, Vali ascended the throne of Kishkinda in accordance with the tradition of primogeniture, and Sugriva became his faithful and resourceful assistant.

Once a fearsome demon named Mayavi came to Kishkinda and challenged Vali to a fight. The Vanara monarch sprang up from his throne and came out, followed closely by Sugriva. If there was to be a fight, Vali intended to engage in a fair one-to-one combat, but Sugriva accompanied him for additional security in case the demon had any accomplices who might attack deviously.

Not knowing the brothers' honourable intentions, Mayavi shrank back in fear when he saw the awesome twosome charging towards him. Realizing that he was no match for their combined might, he turned around and fled.

Vali, knowing that the demon would disrupt the peace in the neighbourhood if he were not taught a lesson, decided to pursue him, and Sugriva followed. Mayavi, trying desperately to shake off the brothers, ducked into a mountain cave that led to a mazelike network of catacombs.

Vali decided to pursue him in the cave's dark cavernous hole and told Sugriva to guard the entrance, lest the demon evade Vali in the maze and try to escape. Sugriva implored Vali to let him join the dangerous subterranean search, but Vali refused and instead repeated his instruction. After his brother vanished into the yawning darkness, Sugriva waited for a long time, peering into the cave as far as the eye could see. He saw nothing and heard nothing till finally the cry of the demon resonated through the cave. Was it a cry of agony or of victory? Sugriva waited, straining and praying to hear some sound of his brother, but the cave remained deathly silent. When the deafening silence went on and on, Sugriva's heart sank as he inferred that his heroic brother had been killed.

Sugriva felt torn between his desire to avenge his brother's death and his duty to protect their kingdom from the deadly demon. If Mayavi came out of the cave, he would be unstoppable. Sugriva pondered: Would I be able to overpower a foe who has already overpowered my more powerful brother? Deciding that discretion was the better part of valour, he devised an alternative strategy. He looked around till he spotted a giant boulder. Straining and sweating and panting, he moved that boulder till it sealed the cave. Feeling reassured that this would keep the demon at bay, Sugriva returned to the kingdom. With a heavy heart, he informed the anxiously waiting courtiers about the demise of their valiant monarch and ordained a period of statewide mourning. After the mourning period ended, the ministers asked Sugriva to take up the role of the king, pointing out the absence of any other qualified heir. Still afflicted by memories of Vali, Sugriva resolved to carry on his brother's legacy and accepted the royal mantle.

From Inseparable to Irreconcilable

A few days later, Vali marched into the palace, his eyes bloodshot. After a long search in the cave, he had found the demon. Being intent on ending the tiresome threat, Vali had wasted no energy in roaring while he slew the screaming demon. When he returned to the cave's entrance, he was vexed to find a huge boulder blocking it. He called out to Sugriva, but got no response. Exhausted by the search and the fight, he couldn't move the boulder. Sugriva's absence and the boulder's presence triggered in him a disconcerting suspicion: Might my trusted brother have connived to lock me in the cave?

Vali needed several days to regain his strength and come up with a plan to move the boulder. The more he struggled, the more his suspicion grew. Surely the boulder was too big to have been moved by the wind or other natural forces. And even if somehow it had been moved naturally, surely it couldn't have so precisely closed the cave.

When Vali finally forced his way out, he raced back to his kingdom, filled with doubts about his brother. When he saw Sugriva seated on the throne, he felt his suspicion confirmed. Enraged, he pounced on Sugriva, whose elation on seeing Vali alive quickly gave way to dismay. Sugriva tried to explain the situation, but Vali was too furious to hear anything and simply pounded Sugriva with his thunderous fists. Sugriva was devastated to see the loathing in his beloved brother's eyes. The thought that his brother had not only suspected but also convicted him hurt Sugriva more than the blows raining down upon him. Having no heart to fight back and hoping he might have a better chance to clarify things later when Vali had cooled down, Sugriva fled from the palace and the kingdom.

Seeing Sugriva flee reinforced Vali's conviction that his brother was guilty. Having thus judged Sugriva as a traitor, Vali's self-righteous mind goaded him to pursue and persecute his brother even in exile, lest he hatch another coup.

The hapless Sugriva fled far and wide, but Vali chased him relentlessly. Finally, Sugriva found refuge right next to Kishkinda—in the Pampa lake area near the hermitage of sage Matanga. Once, in a power-intoxicated show of strength, Vali had flung far away the carcass of Dundubhi, a demon he had killed. The blood from that carcass had fallen on Matanga's sacrificial arena, thus desecrating it. The angered sage, desiring to check Vali's hubris, cursed the monkey to die if he ever entered the vicinity of the hermitage.

In the safe haven created by Matanga's curse, Sugriva lived in an uneasy peace, always fearfully looking out for any assassins Vali might send. As Vali's hostility showed no sign of abating, Sugriva gradually lost all hope of reconciliation. The two inseparable brothers had now become irreconcilable.

Attribution Error

Both Sugriva and Vali arrived at mistaken inferences—Sugriva about Vali's death and Vali about Sugriva's treachery. If we consider the information available to them, they had both made reasonable inferences. The difference between them was that Sugriva had little opportunity to test his inference—the possibility of Mayavi coming out was too hazardous. But Vali had abundant opportunity to test his inference—being stronger, he could afford to give Sugriva a hearing. Moreover, Sugriva was no untrustworthy demon, but was his upright brother, a brother who had served him faithfully as a right-hand man for many years. Sugriva, because of both his relationship and his track record, deserved a proper hearing before being judged. Unfortunately, Vali was too sure of his reading of the situation and felt no need to seek any clarification.

Vali succumbed to a common human error, which psychologists call an attribution error. When we see others behave in an inappropriate way, we tend to attribute that behaviour to internal character flaws, not external extenuating circumstances. Thus, when we see others overeating, we judge them as gluttons. But when we ourselves overeat, we tend to be much more charitable in attribution, sometimes thinking "I had not eaten for so long" or "I will never overeat after this."

We succumb to attribution errors because of a dangerous combination of haste and overconfidence. When faced with the unexpected, we want to understand it quickly; and once we come to an understanding, we hold on to it.

But if our thinking is sound, we will consider the possibility that we may be wrong. After all, the ways in which things happen in the world are complex. And even more complex are the ways in which people think. So determining what makes them behave in particular ways is not easy. Yet when we know something about others, we presume that we know enough to figure out their behaviour—a presumption that often blinds us to our biases and blunders. Rather than falling prey to such presumptions and arriving at snap judgments, we can do better justice to our intelligence by giving others the benefit of doubt and open-mindedly hearing their side of the story.

Due to his haste and overconfidence, Vali succumbed to judging Sugriva without understanding—a surefire recipe for ruining relationships. And sure enough, their relationship soon lay ruined.

Rama's Intervention—Martial and Verbal

Fast-forward to several years: Rama entered the scene and entered into an alliance with Sugriva. As a part of their pact, he promised to correct the wrongs that Vali had done to Sugriva. At Rama's behest, Sugriva challenged Vali to a fight. And when the two brothers were fighting, Rama, after an initial abortive attempt, shot Vali with a lethal arrow.

We may question the morality of Rama's action, as did Vali himself while lying on the ground, mortally wounded. In reply, Rama gave various reasons centred on the point that a sinful aggressor can be killed by any means. Vali had committed multiple acts of aggression against his own brother—attacked with murderous intention, stripped him of all his wealth and even taken Sugriva's wife, Ruma, as his own wife. For an elder brother to seize the wife of his younger brother was a grievous sin, almost akin to incest. Due to all this unwarranted aggression, Rama declared that Vali deserved nothing less than capital punishment.

The analysis of this reasoning can be an article in itself. For our present purpose, it should suffice that Vali found the reasoning convincing. If the plaintiff in a case of perceived injustice pronounces after due discussion and deliberation that no injustice was done, we too can accept that pronouncement. After all, the plaintiff knows more and feels more than us.

After making his case, Rama deferred the judgment to Vali: "If you think I have acted wrongly, I will withdraw the arrow and restore your life and strength right now."

Vali, his hubris destroyed doubly by Rama's arrow piercing his chest and Rama's arrow-like words piercing his presumptions, pondered his actions and recognized their wrongness. He humbly replied that despite his many misdeeds, he had been causelessly blessed to get the priceless opportunity of dying in the auspicious presence of Rama—an opportunity he didn't want to pass over just for a longer life. He further confessed that for long he too had felt he might have wronged Sugriva, but his pride hadn't allowed him to act on, or even voice, that feeling.

Deathbed Reconciliation

With his last few breaths, Vali solaced his sobbing wife, Tara, and his grieving son, Angada. He asked them to hold no grudges towards Sugriva, but to live peaceably under his shelter. Then he turned towards Sugriva, requesting him to bear no malice towards Tara and Angada, but instead care for them.

Seeking forgiveness from his brother and wanting to make amends, Vali took out the jewelled necklace that Indra had given him. That celestial necklace came with the blessing of protecting the life of its wearer. In fact, it was this necklace that had kept Vali alive for so long even after being mortally wounded by Rama's arrow. What father wouldn't desire such armour for his son? Just as Indra had given the necklace to his son, Vali too would have been entirely justified in giving it to his son. But he gave it to Sugriva, thus expressing through his actions the deep remorse he had not the energy or the time to express in words. As soon as the necklace slipped out from Vali's hands, his soul slipped out of his body.

Having heard his brother's heart-wrenching words and seeing him fall back, motionless and silent, Sugriva broke down. This was the elder brother he had known and loved and missed for so long, and would now miss forever. Being overwhelmed with regret for having instigated the killing of such a brother, Sugriva censured himself and resolved to atone for his sin of fratricide by ending his life with that of his brother.

Rama and Lakshmana consoled Sugriva with gentle words, reminding him of his duty to his family and his citizens. Sugriva pulled himself together, ordered the grieving monkeys to arrange for a royal funeral for their deceased king, and began a second period of mourning for his brother.

AAA: Three Steps to Reconciliation

The story of Sugriva and Vali defies simplistic contours of good versus evil. Both brothers were virtuous, but they were ripped apart for life due to one unfortunate misjudgment by the more powerful, more impetuous sibling. What could have been a happy story of fraternal affection became, due to one unclarified misunderstanding, an unhappy story of fraternal animosity that ended in heartbreaking fratricide. Thankfully, their unhappiness was reduced by Rama's intervention, which brought about a pre-mortem reconciliation.

We too can reduce the unhappiness in our relationships by internalizing the critical lesson from this story—never judge without understanding. And if we have already judged others without understanding them, we can seek reconciliation, as did Vali. We can tread the path to reconciliation using the three As: Acknowledge, Apologize, Amend.

Acknowledge: In our relationships that have gone sour, we can honestly introspect and humbly hear from others to check if we might have been more at error than we have believed. If we come to know of our error, we need to acknowledge it, as did Vali after hearing from Rama.

Apologize: Just as arrogant words of judgment can hurt, humble words of rapprochement can heal. We can take huge steps in rebuilding relationships by apologizing, like Vali, for the wrongs we have done, knowingly or unknowingly.

Amend: Actions speak louder than words. Just as Vali gave his necklace to Sugriva, we can do whatever is best possible under the circumstances to correct, or at least mitigate, the consequences of our misjudgment.

Vali required the jolting arrival of death to put aside his pride and make up for his misjudgment. If we meditate on his story and learn from it, we can make up long before such an extreme jolt.

CHAPTER TWELVE

Sugriva-Lakshmana: Comfort—Material and Transcendental

On the spiritual path, adversity is a well-known challenge, but paradoxically, prosperity can be an even greater challenge. While misery can threaten our faith, pleasure can deaden our sense of purpose.

Comfort Breeds Complacency

The Ramayana illustrates how prosperity may become a challenge through the story of Sugriva, the simian-hero who had been unfairly exiled by his brother, Vali, due to a misunderstanding. During the exile, after all his attempts at reconciliation with his brother had failed, he formed an alliance with Rama, who himself had been exiled from his kingdom Ayodhya and was searching for his abducted wife, Sita. Rama helped Sugriva right the wrong and gain the kingdom. In return, Sugriva promised to help Rama find Sita.

By the time Sugriva was enthroned as the king, the rainy season had started. The four months of rains made travelling impossible. So Rama and Sugriva agreed to wait for the rainy season to end before they began the search for Sita. During the waiting period, Sugriva invited Rama to stay in his kingdom in a royal palace. But Rama, wanting to be true to the terms of his fourteen-year exile, stayed in a cave outside the kingdom.

During this four-month period, Sugriva found himself amidst prodigious creature comforts—comforts that he had long been deprived of during his exile. And he unwittingly lost himself in sensual revelry, forgetting all about his promise to Rama.

Time passed and the rainy season ended. Feeling concerned, Rama spoke to Lakshmana, "O brother, I see no sign of Sugriva making any arrangements to find Sita. Please go to the monkey kingdom and take stock of the situation." Lakshmana departed promptly. On his way to Kishkinda, Lakshmana contemplated what he thought was Sugriva's ingratitude and became increasingly incensed till he was seething with anger. Seeing his fury, the monkey-guards became alarmed and scurried off to the palace to alert their king.

Meanwhile, Sugriva hadn't remained entirely inactive—he had been jolted into activity by his vigilant counsellors, his wise wife, Tara, and his able minister, Hanuman. When the rains had started lessening, they had reminded Sugriva of his promise, and he had immediately ordered that monkeys be summoned from far and wide so that they could join the search. But after this brief phase of dutifulness, Sugriva was once again sucked into indulgence by his surrounding luxuries.

When Lakshmana entered Sugriva's chambers and saw the signs of sensual revelry, he exploded. "O Sugriva, ingratitude is the greatest of sins. Condemned are the ingrates who enjoyed themselves while neglecting their promises to their friends." While Sugriva was mortified and could barely speak, Tara intervened and pacified Lakshmana with gentle words, saying, "Please excuse Sugriva for his actions. Even great sages have, at times, fallen prey to temptations, leave alone a monkey who has been long deprived of pleasures and is suddenly surrounded by them." Knowing the root reason for Lakshmana's anger—the apparent absence of any plan to search for Sita—she assured him, "O Lakshmana, powerful monkeys from far and wide are already on their way to Kishkinda; they will soon be sent in various directions to find Sita." On hearing this, Lakshmana became pacified.

Sugriva faced another temptation just before the climactic war between Rama and Ravana. The demon-king with characteristic cunning tried to engineer a split in his opponents. He sent messengers secretly to Sugriva with gifts, stating that the vanaras and the *rakshasas* had no enmity with each other. He further offered Sugriva a favourable pact of mutual assistance if he withdrew his forces from the fray. Living in an austere military camp and being fixed in Rama's service, Sugriva felt not in the least tempted. He rejected the allurement declaring that Rama's enemy was his enemy too.

Subtle Erosion of Devotion

Comforts often erode our devotion subtly. If some miscreants attacked a dam explicitly, security forces would spring into action to counter them and protect the dam. But if those miscreants caused a tiny leakage, most observers may not even notice it—and the water seeping through that leakage may eventually bring down the entire dam.

Similarly, if the forces of illusion came straight out and tempted us with immoral, anti-devotional indulgences, we would probably reject such temptations. But when those forces attack using the weapon of comfort, their attack doesn't make us openly reject God—it just makes us push him down our priority list as comforts rise up on that list.

We may acquire worldly resources for God's service and might even use them for that purpose initially. But gradually we may start indulging in them till the original purpose is forgotten and abandoned—not because of any explicit anti-devotional intention on our part but simply because our increasing sense of complacency has subtly eroded our devotional determination.

Such subtle erosion can be countered by the

practice of austerity. While adversity involves imposed deprivation of material things, austerity involves their voluntary renunciation. Austerity can sharpen our spiritual purposefulness, as illustrated in an incident from the Mahabharata.

When the Pandavas were living in the forest, during one of the later phases of their exile, they ascended through the Himalayas to the heavenly arena where Kuvera, the treasurer of the gods, had his gardens. That great god invited them to stay there for as long as they desired. The Pandavas were technically still in forest exile, but their stay in this heavenly forest was far more comfortable than their austere life in earthly forests.

But after staying there for some time, Bhima and Arjuna approached Yudhishthira and urged him to return to the earthly forest. They both felt that staying amidst comfort would make them forget the atrocities perpetrated against them, deaden their martial spirit, and leave them unprepared for confronting the wily Kauravas, who had 'wrongfully seized their kingdom.

The Pandavas hoped to regain their kingdom non-confrontationally, but they were no Pollyannas—they knew that Duryodhana was driven by an inveterate envy for them, so he would be unlikely to settle for any compromise. So they needed to be prepared for the war, both in spirit and in resources. Yudhishthira agreed with the reasoning of his two heroic brothers and they soon descended to the austere life on earthly forests.

Externally the situations and responses of Sugriva

and the Pandavas were radically different. Sugriva had regained his kingdom, whereas the Pandavas had lost theirs. Further, Sugriva had forgotten his obligation to the Lord, whereas the Pandavas wanted to remember their duty—they wanted their kingdom so that by ruling it according to their dharma, they could serve and glorify the Lord. Still, despite these dissimilarities, both incidents share the same underlying theme—indulgence in comforts can erode our sense of purpose. Sugriva lost that sense because of immersion in comforts and pleasures. The Pandavas, on the other hand, protected themselves from such a loss by giving up the comforts that might have made them complacent. Indeed, austerity can often serve as an insurance against complacency.

Technological Paradise?

In our time, comforts come to us primarily through technology. It often fills us with a sense of godless omnipotence—we are led to believe that we can just by clicking a few buttons get whatever we want. Thus, we are allured towards a technological paradise that is touted, overtly or covertly, as a superior substitute to any spiritual paradise.

But while we may temporarily control more and more external things by clicking a few buttons, we find ourselves being increasingly unable to control, by any button, the world within us. Our minds and our emotions become increasingly disorderly. As Martin Luther King Jr. put it, "The means by which we live have outdistanced the ends for which we live. Our scientific power has outrun our spiritual power. We have guided missiles and misguided men."

In contemporary times, the more humanity is distancing itself from God in the hope of a hi-tech paradise, the more it is being overwhelmed by mental problems. Indeed, mental health problems have been declared by the WHO to be the greatest health challenge of the current century.

Nonetheless, the bhakti tradition is not Luddite; both the Ramayana and the Mahabharata feature sophisticated weapons. Bhakti wisdom explains that the problem is not the prevalence of technology; the problem is the absence of God consciousness—an absence that is aggravated by the reductionistic worldview that accompanies modern technology.

Reductionism is the idea that complicated things can be explained by breaking them down into their components. While this idea works for machines, some people extrapolate it to all of reality. When used in this sense, reductionism refers to the belief system that reduces everything in the universe to the movements of atomic particles acting according to impersonal laws. Such a belief system, by denying the existence of any divine intelligence guiding the processes of nature, makes us see technological wizardry as the product of humanity, not the gift of divinity. Those advocating such reductionism forget that all technological products that humanity has developed—be they planes for commuting or phones for communicating—are based on pre-existing natural principles such as the laws of motion or the semiconductor effect. And these natural principles don't originate in human intelligence; they originate ultimately in God's intelligence. Therefore, for the discerning observer, every technological success is not just a testimony to human intelligence but also a tribute to divine intelligence.

To cultivate such discernment, we need to perform the conscious austerity of fixing our mind on God through direct devotional practices such as meditation and scriptural study. When we habituate ourselves to such direct God consciousness, we will be able to see the spiritual underlying the technological, thereby protecting ourselves from complacency.

Spiritualization, Not Rejection

Bhakti asks not for the rejection of the world but for connection with its source, God. While some renouncer traditions do see the world primarily as a place of entanglement, the bhakti tradition sees it more positively— as a resource to serve him. Everything material and spiritual comes from him, so it is intrinsically connected with him as his energy and is meant to be used in his service.

Therefore, the bhakti tradition doesn't romanticize adversity or demonize prosperity—it urges us to utilize whatever circumstance we find ourselves in. Adversity in and of itself is not spiritually beneficial; extreme adversity can make both basic material subsistence and basic spiritual practice difficult. And prosperity in and of itself is not spiritually harmful; a reliable and comfortable provision of material needs can free the mind from survival anxiety to ponder higher spiritual truths and ultimately the highest spiritual truth—God.

Though the kingdom had induced forgetfulness in Sugriva, none of his counsellors ask him to renounce his material comforts. Instead, they ask him to revive his remembrance of Rama's benedictions and render practical service to him. Similarly, we can see whatever comforts we have as God's gifts. Rather than seeing them as agents of temptation and illusion, we can see them as expressions of God's kindness and thus feel inspired to serve him better. We can think, "As God has given me such a comfortable situation in which to serve him, let me increase and intensify my service to him—increase in quantity by using these resources to spread his glories, and intensify in quality by cherishing his remembrance more."

Tara, Hanuman, and Lakshmana, all reminded Sugriva of his obligation and helped him correct his deviation. Similarly, we too need friends and guides who can remind us of our obligation to the Lord, especially when we start deviating from it.

Spiritual association is vital for preserving our sense of devotional purposefulness. To the extent we keep ourselves in such association and hear spiritual messages therein—as Sugriva did—to that extent we will be safe, even if we are amidst worldly comforts. We won't be caught by the material, but will see beyond the material to the supreme spiritual reality, the Lord of our heart, thus staying connected with him. And that inner connection is life's supreme comfort, the one comfort that will never become pale and stale, the one comfort that will always shelter us, and the one comfort that far from breeding complacency will raise our devotion to greater fervency.

CHAPTER THIRTEEN

Angada-Hanuman: Unity—Within and Without

The Ramayana features many intriguing group dynamics, among human groups, monkey groups, demon groups, and even human-monkey groups. Divisive and cohesive forces are graphically evident in the group of monkeys that had gone south in search of Sita.

The Search and the Schism

The backstory is that the monkey monarch, Sugriva, had organized his leading monkeys into four groups and instructed them to go in the four directions to search for Sita. The search parties were asked to return within a month with latecomers liable to severe punishment. Among the groups, the south-bound group was most likely to locate Sita—Ravana had been seen carrying her southwards. This group had as leaders three great monkey generals: Angada, Hanuman, and Jambavan. Rama gave Hanuman a signet that he was to show to Sita on finding her; the signet would assure her that its bearer was an authorized messenger of Rama.

The group's three leaders had different things to commend them—age, lineage, and grace. By age, Jambavan was the senior-most and was accorded due deference. But his age had decreased his physical prowess. By lineage, Angada was a valiant prince, being the son of the previous monkey monarch, Vali. But he was young, impetuous, and inexperienced. By grace, Hanuman had received from the gods many extraordinary powers. But those powers had made him, when he was still a mischievous child, into an innocent menace for forest sages. So, those sages had cursed him to forget his powers till he was reminded of them at a later, more opportune moment. Being thus forgetful, Hanuman hadn't, till this point in the Ramayana, done anything extraordinarily heroic.

The south-bound group searched vigorously for over six weeks, braving many dangers, but couldn't find any clue to Sita's whereabouts. And amidst the consequent disappointment, concealed tensions within the group came to the fore.

Their search for Sita having drawn a blank, the disheartened monkeys discussed their next strategy:

Should they keep searching? Or should they return, report their failure, and seek further orders? Their predicament triggered Angada's residual suspicions about Sugriva, and he voiced those suspicions to others, "O monkeys, if we go back, Sugriva will order that we be executed. He will hold us culpable for failing to find Sita and for returning late." Noticing that the monkeys were shocked, he forcefully continued, "What else can you expect from a person who conspired to kill his own brother? I feel that fasting to death in the forest will be better than returning only to be executed in disgrace in front of our loved ones."

On hearing Angada's apprehension, the monkeys responded variously, till they split into two groups. One group agreed with Angada and resolved to fast to death. The other group sided with Hanuman, who underscored Sugriva's fairness and assured that no one would be penalized for the delay.

Seismic Fault Lines in Relationships

Were Angada's doubts about Sugriva justified? Yes and no. Sugriva had undoubtedly arranged for killing Vali. But he had done so not because he craved power, but because Vali had left him with no alternative. Vali had blown out of proportion an unfortunate misunderstanding with Sugriva. Without giving his brother any chance for clarifying things, Vali had driven him to the forest, stripped him of all royal status and taken his brother's wife for himself. Worse still, Vali had chased Sugriva far and wide with murderous intent. He had given up only when Sugriva sought refuge near a hermitage that Vali couldn't approach due to a sage's curse. Sugriva had tried repeatedly to reconcile with Vali, but Vali had rebuffed, rebuked, and threatened him. Seeing no other way to guarantee his life and regain his family, Sugriva had felt constrained to arrange for Vali's death.

Significantly, Vali had reconciled with Sugriva moments before his death. He had sought Sugriva's forgiveness and had requested him to treat Tara (Vali's wife) and Angada kindly. Moreover, Vali had requested Tara and Angada to stay under Sugriva's shelter and serve him as they had served Vali earlier. So the animosity between the two brothers had been fully dissolved before Vali's death.

Even after gaining the kingdom, Sugriva had shown no glee. Quite the opposite. Vali's death had filled him with such deep remorse that he had desired to enter the funeral pyre with his brother's corpse. He had been dissuaded only by the words of his well-wishers, Rama and Lakshmana, who had reminded him of, among other things, his duty to his citizens. After reluctantly ascending the throne, Sugriva had carefully honoured his dying brother's request by being consistently considerate towards Angada.

Moreover, presently, Sugriva had sent them on a mission to serve Rama. And that virtuous prince would certainly not allow the unjust execution of anyone, leave alone the prince.

Unfortunately, none of this reasoning could allay Angada's suspicions, disheartened as he was at their unfruitful search. He chose, unilaterally, the extreme measure of suicidal self-mortification.

It's revealing that Angada's suspicions came to the fore when their mission met with a reversal that bordered on failure. The mind often magnifies problems. Bhagavad-gita (06.06) cautions that our mind is presently our enemy. One of the ways it acts inimically is by distorting our perception—sometimes it trivializes big problems and sometimes it magnifies small problems. Sometimes, when faced with one big problem, it becomes so pessimistic and paranoid as to imagine other problems to be bigger than what they are. Thus, at times, the mind escalates minor relationship issues.

Relationships are often so subtle and multi-level that some small tensions can exist even in the closest relationships. But the mind transforms these tensions into seismic fault lines that, if unresolved, can give rise to a relationship-shattering quake.

A Predator Turns Benefactor

Hanuman found himself in a delicate situation. Angada, the prince and heir, was leading the monkeys to mass suicide. Moreover, he was voicing serious accusations against the king. Still, Hanuman exhibited maturity in not going off the handle and counter-accusing Angada of treason. He understood that the prince's words came from a hurting heart—he was still a youth, a bereaved son who had unexpectedly lost his father just a few months ago and who was now burdened by his failure in the leadership responsibility he had been entrusted with. That he had even accepted such a responsibility was laudable. With gentle words and sound arguments, Hanuman tried to persuade Angada. But, despite his best efforts, he couldn't make any headway.

Often when we do the best we can, God helps us to do what we can't. And his help may well come in the least expected ways—sometimes in ways that don't look like help at all. For the arguing monkeys, divine help came in a scary form.

While the monkeys' talks had come to an impasse, suddenly a giant vulture emerged from a nearby cave. On beholding the monkeys sitting in a posture meant for fasting till death, he declared, "Providence has been very kind to me today. I will soon feast on these monkeys."

The monkeys were dismayed to see the giant vulture. The lamenting Angada became even more morose. Turning to a monkey sitting next to him, he said, "Alas! Has this vulture been sent by providence to punish us for failing to serve Rama? Seeing him reminds me of another vulture, Jatayu. Just as Jatayu had died while trying in vain to stop Ravana from kidnapping Sita, we too seem fated to die unsuccessfully after failing in our service to Rama."

On hearing the mention of Jatayu, the vulture froze. Recovering after a few moments, he asked, "O monkeys, did you just mention Jatayu? Did you say that he had died? Please tell me what happened to him. I am Jatayu's elder brother, Sampati."

Relieved and intrigued, Angada told the story of how Jatayu had attained martyrdom while trying to stop Ravana from abducting Sita. Sampati cried in agony and anger, "Fie on me. Despite being the elder one, I failed to protect Jatayu. And so pitiable is my condition that I can't even avenge his death because I no longer have wings."

Seeing that the monkeys were hearing sympathetically, he told them how he had lost his wings. "Long ago, when Jatayu and I were young and impetuous, we decided to fly till the sun. When we got close, sun's heat started scorching us, so I shaded Jatayu with my wings. The heat burnt my wings, and I fell to the earth, wingless and separated from Jatayu. While I was lying there, helpless and sorrowful, a sage named Chandrama solaced me by providing me knowledge of my eternal soul. He assured me that good would come out my predicament—this adversity would give me an opportunity to serve the Lord in one of his future descents."

As Sampati fell silent, Angada contemplated his words. A thought lit his heart with hope and he asked Sampati, "You have flown far and wide across the universe. Do you know where Ravana's kingdom is located?" Hearing his question, Sampati perked up. He spoke excitedly, "Chandrama's words have come true. Rama is God descended on earth. And you monkeys are Rama's servants. By pointing you to Ravana's kingdom, I can serve Rama. And Rama will surely punish the demon who slew Jatayu. Thus, I can help in avenging my brother. O monkeys, Ravana's kingdom, Lanka, is an island in the ocean that we can see to our south."

Becoming contemplative, he continued, "Several months ago, I saw a beautiful woman carried southward through the sky by Ravana." Becoming animated, he drew himself to his full height and continued, "O monkeys, age has weakened my body, but not my sight." Focusing his eyes across the ocean, he announced, "Sita is right now there in Ravana's kingdom, Lanka."

The monkeys were elated. Their mutual differences forgotten, the two groups of monkeys jubilantly embraced each other and started celebrating. After they calmed down, they began planning their next move. Angada too put aside his suspicions. His devotion for Rama had always been strong. Even when doubts about Sugriva had overwhelmed him, he had still wanted to serve Rama. Now that an avenue to succeed in his service to Rama had opened, he was able to push back those doubts.

After this incident, Angada never succumbed to similar doubts about his uncle. In the climactic war, he fought faithfully under Sugriva, heroically felling many dreadful demons. And the other monkeys too never mentioned Angada's accusations. Leaving the past behind them, they worked unitedly and successfully in Rama's service.

A Big Problem Solved through a Bigger Problem

The specifics of this story may not seem relevant to us when we in our daily lives face divisive tensions. But if we look beyond those specifics to generic patterns, we can discern four stages that may well resonate with our experience:

- A group of strong individuals come together for a challenging cause.
- A reversal aggravates underlying tensions, creating a schism.
- A bigger problem appears, bringing the group together.
- In working unitedly, the group tackles the bigger problem along with the original problem.

The turning point for the monkeys was an incidental, distress-triggered reference to Jatayu. Significantly, their comparing themselves with Jatayu revealed that they were still committed to Rama. And that casual expression of their devotion turned out to be life-saving and mission-saving. Hearing Jatayu's name, Sampati turned from predator to benefactor, and told them Sita's whereabouts.

Still, even that turning point had initially looked like a worsening point. Sampati had seemed not god-sent, but devil-sent, being bent on devouring the monkeys. But despite appearances, behind the scenes, things were moving by divine arrangement to assist them. And when they persevered, that assistance manifested.

When we face problems while serving the Lord, we can't know when and how a turning point may come. Even if things seem grim, we never lose till we lose hope. And even if we lose hope, our Lord doesn't. He can work in the most inconceivable ways to give us hope and direction.

Whenever we work together, as we often need to for achieving anything big, differences of opinion are inevitable. To survive and succeed amidst such differences, we need to focus on the cause that brings us together, not the conditions and conditionings that push us apart. If we can voluntarily maintain this focus, that is the best. But if we somehow lose focus, problems seem to balloon. Those problems compel us to choose: will we correct course by uniting around the common cause or will we be ripped apart by our differences?

The best common cause is the cause of devotion to God, for he is the well-wisher of everyone, as Bhagavad-gita (05.29) states. And he engages his devotees as agents of his wisdom, helping them find their way through obstacles.

Interactions and Inner Actions

Successful teamwork rests on not just the interactions between individuals but also the inner actions within the individuals' minds. This is seen from how Angada's internal suspicion caused external dissension. Pertinently, devotion can unify us not only with others, but also with ourselves. That is, devotion can unite our present consciousness with our pure consciousness as spiritual beings, as parts of God.

We have a lower side that prods us towards shortsighted actions. And we have a higher side that inspires us towards nobler, farsighted actions that are truer to our essential nature and core values. Devotion activates and strengthens our higher side, gradually elevating and uniting our self-conception with our spiritual self.

However, our lower side tends to minimize devotion, making us believe that worldly exigencies are far more important and urgent than any spiritual cause. And as such exigencies keep coming, one after another, they leave us spiritually disoriented and decentred. Thus, we become vulnerable to divisive influences that aggravate worldly exigencies, thereby trapping us in a circle of spiritual distraction and worldly obsession. To avoid this trap, we need to use our intelligence, sharpened by regular study of scripture, to keep our devotion at the centre of our heart and our relationships.

When we keep ourselves devotionally grounded, we get the inner security to act maturely in outer relationships. We can firmly resist unwarranted suspicions and non-confrontationally resolve warranted concerns. And adversities that could rupture unity can instead strengthen it if we see them as spurs for focusing on God and the common cause of serving him.

Hanuman's Journey to Lanka: Overcoming Obstacles through Devotional Purposefulness

Among the most visually dramatic events in the Ramayana is Hanuman's flight across the ocean to Lanka, the stronghold of the demon-king Ravana who had abducted Sita. During his aerial journey, Hanuman's thoughts and actions when encountering various obstacles can guide us when we face challenges.

Let Reflections Reinforce Action

When Hanuman leapt off the Indian coastline, he fixed his mind on Rama. He remembered Rama's grief-stricken yet hope-filled words during their last meeting when Rama had given him a signet ring to give to Sita. Rama had not given any such token to anyone else in any of the search parties sent in the four directions to search for Sita. Rama's handing that ring to Hanuman reflected his confidence that Hanuman would find Sita.

Remembering Rama's confidence in him, Hanuman felt increasingly energized to reach Lanka as fast as possible. The wind-god, the celestial father of Hanuman, wanted to aid his son who was performing such an extraordinary service to their Lord. Accordingly, the wind started flowing from behind Hanuman, thus helping him move faster.

As Hanuman flew, beholding the vast ocean stretching out in all directions below him reminded him of the potency of Rama's names. He thought, "The sacred scriptures declare that by chanting the Lord's names, one can cross over the entire ocean of material existence—what, then, would be the difficulty in crossing over one ocean within that material existence?"

Seeing shoals of aquatics moving about in the ocean, Hanuman thought of how the other vanaras (celestial monkeys) in his party were praying for his success—and not just praying but also performing austerities. When he was preparing to take-off for Lanka, the other vanaras had told him that till he returned, they all would perform yogic meditation; they would stand on one foot, praying that the merits of their austerity assist Hanuman in his mission.

As he remembered those for whom he was working and those with whom he was working, his inspiration increased and his determination deepened. With his reflections thus energizing his actions, Hanuman sped through the sky towards Lanka.

Whenever we do anything challenging, we need to ensure that our thoughts support us, not sabotage us. If we conscientiously contemplate the things that inspire us, not the things that dishearten us, our contemplations can work in tandem with our actions.

Don't Let the Good Come in the Way of the Best

When Hanuman was speeding above the ocean, he suddenly found a mountain rising in front of him. The personified mountain, a venerable elderly person, spoke to Hanuman, "I am Mainaka. O monkey, you are on a mission to serve Rama. I was a friend to his noble father, Dashratha and I want to serve Rama by serving you, a dedicated servant of Rama. O Hanuman, please rest on the mountain for some time before continuing on your tiring flight."

For Hanuman, reciprocating with Mainaka's desire to serve Rama would not have been wrong—far from it, it would have been proper etiquette. Devotees are expected to be courteous with everyone, what to speak of with other devotees.

But Hanuman had a mission far more urgent than resting or socializing. He knew how much Rama was distressed in separation from Sita, and he could also imagine how Sita would be pining in separation from her

Lord. Now that he was so close to reaching Sita, he didn't want to lose even one moment.

Moreover, Sugriva had asked the search parties to return within a month. Hanuman and his party had already been searching for more than a month. He didn't want to do anything that would delay him further.

And yet Hanuman didn't have the heart to reject the service that Mainaka was so kindly offering. After all, Mainaka was a pious soul, devoted to the same Lord to whom Hanuman was devoted.

So, he lowered himself from his aerial trajectory and touched the mountain, thus offering it his respects. Rising again, he explained, "O Mainaka, I am on an urgent service. Rama is in agony, awaiting news of Sita. By touching you, I have accepted your hospitality. Pray give me your permission so that I may continue on my mission." Pleased with Hanuman's untiring eagerness to serve Rama, Mainaka gladly gave permission.

The Lord states in Bhagavad-gita (09.26) that when he is offered anything with devotion, he accepts even the simplest of offerings because he focuses on the devotion with which it is offered. Hanuman, as a devotee of that same Lord, accepted Mainaka's devotion while ensuring that in practice his own service was not delayed. Thus, Hanuman expertly did both—he honoured etiquette and stayed fixed in his purpose.

When we are rendering an important and difficult service, we may be offered comforts by those wanting to assist us. We may be inclined to enjoy those comforts as due rewards for our hard work. But if we keep our purpose foremost, we won't be swayed.

Simultaneously, we need to be careful not to go to the other extreme either. We may be tempted to reject those comforts as an exhibition of our renunciation. Hanuman's example reminds us to be courteous, appreciating the other person's intention of service, even when we have to say no.

Hanuman's declining Mainaka's offer also illustrates that the good is often the greatest enemy of the best. If we have to choose between the bad and the best, we will naturally choose the best—at least we won't be confused about what to choose, even if our conditioning make that choice difficult to implement. But when we have to choose between the good and the best, the mind's rationalizations can delude us into preferring the good.

By nourishing our intelligence regularly through scriptural study, we can keep our eyes fixed on the best.

When we have a yes for the most important thing burning within us, we will get the conviction to say no to less important things.

Know which Battles to Fight and which to Skip

When Hanuman flew on, he soon found his path blocked by a gigantic creature who identified herself as the demoness, Surasa. Actually, she was a goddess, the mother of the Nagas and the daughter of Daksha. She had been asked by the gods to test Hanuman, specifically to test his *bala* (strength) and *buddhi* (intelligence), two resources he would need in abundance if he were to succeed in Lanka.

Opening her mouth wide, Surasa told Hanuman, "I am going to devour you. You have no chance to escape because I have been blessed by Brahma that any creature going by this area will have to enter my mouth."

Initially, when Hanuman had seen this fearsome demoness with her deadly mouth wide open, he had been about to attack. But on hearing her speak, he changed tack. He requested her, "I am on an urgent mission to deliver Rama's message to his abducted wife, Sita. Please let me deliver that message. On my return journey, I promise to enter your mouth." When she remained unrelenting, he told her, "I will enter your mouth if you can make it big enough to accommodate me." Saying this, he expanded his size. When the demoness made her mouth bigger than him, he made his body bigger still. No matter how big she made her mouth, Hanuman kept making himself bigger still. Both of them repeatedly exhibited their extraordinary shape-changing abilities.

When Hanuman saw that this competition of size expansion was just going on and on, he reversed his strategy—he suddenly decreased his body to a small size. He entered into Surasa's mouth and, before she could close her cavernous mouth, he slipped out. Folding his hands in front of her, he told her, "I have honoured Brahma's benediction by entering into your mouth. Please let me proceed now." Pleased with him, she revealed her true identity and purpose, and blessed him to move on.

Hanuman thus passed the test of the gods with flying colours. He demonstrated his strength and intelligence—strength by expanding his body to phenomenal dimensions and intelligence by expertly honouring Brahma's benediction while persevering in his purpose.

Here, Hanuman intelligently chose his battles. As a warrior who loved a good fight, he could have seen Surasa's challenge as a spur to fight. But he expertly put first things first. Instead of getting into a needless and possibly endless confrontation, he took the humble position by decreasing his size, and moved on with his mission. For Hanuman, proving his own greatness was not as important as progressing on his great mission.

We too need to be similarly intelligent in choosing our battles. Amidst conflicts, we need to discern which issues to hold on to and which to let go. Many things may be wrong around us, and we may feel that we need to set them all right. But we are finite beings with finite time, energy, and resources. If we try to fight every single battle that chances across our way, we will keep fighting endlessly, draining ourselves completely, and not doing even the things which we could have done.

In our interactions with our loved ones, we may find ourselves getting into a heated argument on an issue that is not particularly important. At such a time, instead of getting sucked into a confrontation, we need to mentally take a step back and get our priorities straight—our relationship is more important than this issue. Our love should free us from the need to be right in every argument.

Knowing that the battle of egos can be endless, we can take the humble position. Humility doesn't mean letting ourselves be trampled on by others—it simply means that we don't let our ego come in the way of our purpose.

When One Door Closes, Look for the Door that Has Opened

While Hanuman was flying on, he suddenly found himself paralyzed. Though he strained to the fullest extent of his phenomenal strength, he couldn't move onwards. Looking down, he saw a hideous demoness looking at him and licking her lips. He understood that she had used her mystic powers to catch his shadow, thereby arresting his progress. As he was considering his options, he found himself being pulled down towards her devouring, gloating mouth. Her plan was to chew Hanuman in her mouth, thereby killing him and feasting on him.

With remarkable presence of mind, Hanuman used the momentum generated by the demonesses pulling him down to keep speeding through her mouth down into her alimentary canal. Before she could even understand what was happening, he went deep into her stomach and started attacking it from within. Eventually, ripping apart her stomach from inside, he emerged, unhurt and victorious. As the demoness fell screaming to her death into the ocean, setting off huge waves, Hanuman flew on.

Simhika can be said to represent envious people who try to pull down the person who is the object of their envy. Just as Simhika caught Hanuman's shadow, the envious catch hold of incidental or inconsequential faults in those who are doing good things, even extraordinary things. But just as the very power with which Simhika pulled Hanuman down ended up becoming a cause of her destruction, the shenanigans of the envious rebound against them.

Sometimes, envious people may create problems for us that are almost impossible to overcome, just as Hanuman found it impossible to move on. Instead of becoming overwhelmed or disheartened, we can keep our wits with us, as did Hanuman. And some way will emerge.

In general, during our life-journey, when one door closes in our face, we may feel frustrated. But instead of glaring at that door, we can start looking for some other door that might be opening. If we let resentment blind us, we will miss the opened door.

The no to a particular door in life is not a no to life. Failures in life don't equate with a failed life. If we keep persevering in our service attitude, striving our best to find some way to serve our Lord, then, no matter how many doors close in our life, some door will soon open somewhere. Bhagavad-gita (18.58) assures that those who stay conscious of the Lord are guided by his grace to overcome all obstacles.

Even if we find ourselves powerless externally, we needn't let ourselves become hopeless internally. If we keep ourselves faithfully hopeful, then that inner power of faith will attract the supreme power of divine grace, revealing a way where none seemed to exist.

Flying on, Hanuman eventually reached Lanka. He saw a huge island with a central fortified city, walled off on all sides. He assumed a small form to discreetly enter into the city. Suddenly, a demoness blocked him. Declaring herself to be Lankini, the guardian of Lanka, she chastised him for trying to sneak in.

As a shrewd warrior, Hanuman could size up the strength of opponents. Assessing Lankini's strength, he slapped her with enough force to knock her down, but not slay her.

Again, his purpose was foremost in his mind. He wanted to find Sita as soon as possible. So, before Lankini could recover from the shock of being felled by a mere monkey whom she had been planning to gleefully devour, Hanuman sped past, entering Lanka.

While trying to figure out how a mere monkey could have overpowered her, Lankini remembered an ancient prophecy—when she would be overcome by a monkey, Lanka would soon be destroyed. With an impending sense of doom, Lankini got up and went to alert Ravana.

Perhaps the most important lesson from Hanuman's adventurous leap to Lanka is his single-minded purposefulness. Rather than letting obstacles deter him, he resourcefully found a way through them.

Similarly, when faced with obstacles, if we stay purpose-conscious instead of becoming obstacle-conscious, the Lord will show us ways to move ahead.

CHAPTER FIFTEEN

Hanuman in Lanka:
A Tail-blazing and Trail-blazing
Adventure in Devotion

F ew missions are as difficult as the mission entrusted to Hanuman, the vanara hero in the Ramayana who comes into his own in the later part of the epic.

When his team of vanaras searching for Sita had been stymied by an unsurpassable ocean, he had to press on single-handedly as he alone had the strength to leap across the ocean and return.

An Ocean of Obstacles

Even after he had crossed the ocean, Hanuman still faced a host of challenges—entering into the heavily guarded city of Lanka; searching for a woman by looking in places frequented by women while maintaining his celibacy; locating Sita among the thousands of people living there; winning her trust so that she would see him as Rama's messenger, not as Ravana's disguised agent; assuring her of Rama's love for her and his determination to come to rescue her; escaping alive from Lanka to inform his colleagues about Sita's whereabouts.

How Hanuman accomplished all these, and actually accomplished much more, is an incredible adventure that comprises the heart of the Sundara-Kanda, the fourth book of the Ramayana. Here we pick up the action after he had entered Lanka. To enter undetected, he assumed a small inconspicuous form. He slipped in unnoticed among the rows of soldiers guarding Lanka's walls. Sneaking in and out of various buildings, he managed to avoid arousing suspicion by his agility and alertness.

Impure Perception, Pure Intention

While sneaking into various houses, especially their inner chambers, Hanuman saw several women in various states of undress. He felt a grave doubt: Was he acting irreligiously by looking at women thus? After due introspection, he concluded that he was not driven by the desire for voyeuristic pleasure; he was motivated purely by the desire to serve Rama by finding Sita. As he had to look for a woman and had to do so discreetly, he had no alternative to looking in women's chambers. Thus, he demonstrated that service may sometimes take the unlikeliest of forms.

After seeing signs of revelry in various palaces in the city, he reached the biggest building, self-evidently Ravana's palace. Therein, on a majestic bed, he saw Ravana asleep and nearby was a beautiful woman, similarly asleep. Thinking that he had found Sita, he started jumping up and down in delight. But soon it struck him that Sita would be grieving because of separation from Rama and wouldn't have given herself up to Ravana—this woman who was sleeping so comfortably in Ravana's house couldn't be Sita.

Feeling chastened, he continued his search through the many palaces.

From Discouragement to Discovery through Determination

Despite searching exhaustively, he couldn't find Sita anywhere. Gloomy thoughts started consuming him. He had come so far and gone through so much to come so far, yet now he seemed doomed to fail. Contemplating what his failure would do to others triggered a mental dystopia. On hearing of his failure, Rama would not be able to maintain his life. If Rama passed away, so would Lakshmana. Seeing the demise of those two princes would similarly fell the citizens of Ayodhya. Sugriva too would give up his life, deeming himself a failure for not keeping his word to help Rama find Sita. With Sugriva's grief-struck death, Kishkinda's citizens too would meet the same fate.

Intriguingly, such dystopian thoughts energized Hanuman. He resolved that rather than be the bearer of bad news that would wreck such devastation, he would keep searching for Sita till his last breath.

Hanuman's resilience demonstrates the power of resolute intention. Life's adversities can knock down even the best among us, but they don't have to keep us down. If our intention is strong enough, that intention will eventually prevail over circumstantial situations and emotions.

Though Hanuman was determined to keep searching for Sita, he was unsure of what to do next—he had already searched the entire city. When we resolutely pursue a worthy cause, forces far beyond ours come to our aid, often in inconceivable ways. While Hanuman was considering his next move, the moon providentially came out from behind the clouds. It revealed to his searching eyes the palace-gardens that he had overlooked while looking through various houses. The thought occurred to him that Sita might have refused to stay in a palace while her Lord was living in a forest and might have insisted on living similarly in the wilderness. Excited, he felt a surge of hope and energy rushing through him.

Bounding quickly to the garden, he searched through it till he noticed a woman of incredible beauty. Dressed in soiled clothes, she was sitting desolately under a tree surrounded by hideous-looking demonesses. While he was observing, he saw Ravana approaching her. The demon was trying to wheedle and threaten her into submission. Overhearing their conversations, Hanuman understood that the object of Ravana's unwanted attention was the object of his search: Sita. He felt delighted on finding her, but his joy was tempered on seeing her plight.

As he watched on, the exasperated Ravana walked away in a huff, after directing harsh parting words at Sita. The demonesses guarding her swarmed around her, speaking threateningly to her, gesticulating towards Ravana, apparently pressuring her to accept his proposition. But Sita remained unmoved and soon the demonesses gave up.

Overcome Mutual Suspicion by Divine Glorification

After the demonesses had withdrawn to a distance, Hanuman crept closer to Sita and started an activity that wins the hearts of devotees—speaking the Lord's glories.

He gave vivid details of Rama's pastimes including intimate details that no one except Rama and Sita knew—details that Rama had uttered when expressing to Hanuman his agony in separation from Sita. Delighted on hearing her Lord being glorified, Sita looked around and spotted the small monkey sitting atop a tree with folded hands. Hanuman jumped down and introduced himself. Though Sita was understandably suspicious, he won her confidence by showing Rama's signet ring. Seeing it, Sita broke down into tears, being overwhelmed with remembrance of her Lord.

The subsequent talk between the servant of Rama and the consort of Rama—both devotees par excellence—is intensely moving. Their fervent remembrances of Rama invoke his intense presence amidst his absence.

Sita told Hanuman, "O Hanuman, when will Rama come and rescue me? The wicked Ravana has threatened to consume me for breakfast if I don't submit to him within one year." On hearing that Sita's life was in danger, Hanuman was alarmed. He told Sita urgently, "Just climb on my back and I will immediately carry you to Rama." In his anxiety, Hanuman forgot that he was still in the form of a small monkey, half the size of Sita, and that she didn't know about his strength. When she voiced the obvious question, "O Hanuman, how will you carry me?" he felt piqued. Expanding his form to towering proportions, he declared, "O Sita, have no doubt. I can easily carry you not just out of Lanka but even across the ocean." Still, Sita expressed another practical concern: "When you try to escape with me, the demons will surely attack you. You will find it difficult to fight with them while carrying me." Seeing Hanuman about to protest, probably to argue that he could still fight, she continued, "Also, I don't wish to be touched by any man other than Rama. When Ravana abducted me, I was helpless. I desire to be rescued by Rama alone." Appreciating her chastity, Hanuman assured her, "As soon as Rama comes to know your whereabouts, he

will come to rescue you." He took her leave and took
with him her message for Rama and his memories of her
unswerving devotion.

Too Busy to be Humiliated

Though his mission of locating Sita was accomplished,
Hanuman felt inspired to do more, much more. Knowing
that a war with Ravana was most likely unavoidable, he
desired to do a reconnaissance mission to assess Lanka's
defensive formations. He also wanted to deter the
demons from war by delivering a grim warning and by
demonstrating the power of Rama's servants.

With this in mind, Hanuman started destroying the
Ashoka vatika, the garden that he had come to know was
Ravana's favourite. The guards tried to stop him and were
soon decimated. So were series of warriors sent by Ravana,
each of successively greater strength, including even his
own son, Aksha. Finally, Ravana's most powerful son,
Indrajita, attacked Hanuman and bound him using the
Brahmastra weapon. Hanuman knew that this formidable
weapon would restrain him only for a short time, and that
he could break free soon at the right time. So, despite
being physically overcome, he was not mentally overcome.
He remained alert and determined to serve Rama.

The bound vanara was soon dragged through the
streets of Lanka with demons mocking and kicking him.
They wanted to humiliate him and demonstrate to Lanka's

citizens the fate that would inevitably befall anyone who dared antagonize Lanka's Lord.

Had Hanuman been foolhardy in provoking the demons? No, he had thought his strategy well. While arrested, he was lying low, fully ready to catch his attackers off guard and wreak havoc in their ranks. More importantly, while being paraded through Lanka's streets, he was too busy to be humiliated. He was keenly observing Lanka's various paths, evaluating their feasibility for launching surprise attacks, should such an eventuality arise.

Hanuman was always focused on serving Rama, irrespective of whether he was flying forcefully across an ocean or was pulled forcibly through a street. Similarly, when we stay fixed in the intention to serve the Lord, even in the midst of adversity, we will find some opportunity to serve, though that service may differ radically from our normal service.

Eventually, Hanuman was brought into Ravana's presence in his court. Despite being bound, humiliated and threatened, Hanuman's first thought on seeing Ravana was revealing: he felt not fear, but grief—not fear that this formidable demon might punish or kill him, but grief that a person with such gifts had wasted his life because of his godlessness; if he had been virtuous, he could have done so much good for the world. A sign of a healthy mind is to see good in everything, even the bad. And a sign of a devotionally healthy mind is to see the potential for service to the Lord in everyone, even those sworn to defy the Lord. Such was the spiritually vibrant consciousness of Hanuman.

On seeing the bound monkey, some of the warriors said, "This vandal deserves to be executed." But Ravana, wanting to first know the intruder's identity and purpose, ordered that he be interrogated.

Wanting time to observe the leading demon commanders carefully, Hanuman initially toyed with his interrogators, claiming innocence. "I am just a monkey. When I felt hungry, I plucked a few fruits, but somehow, a few trees fell in the process. And suddenly I found myself being attacked by the demons. To protect myself, I fought against those bent on killing me."

When the interrogators grilled Hanuman about why he had come to Lanka, Hanuman ended his toying with them. "I am a servant of Sugriva, the king of the Vanaras, and I have come here as a messenger of Rama, the peerless prince of Ayodhya." Addressing Ravana directly, he spoke sternly, "O demon, by abducting Sita, you have courted death. Return her to Rama forthwith, or you will soon be dead." When Ravana and other demons mocked Rama as a pauper who had been exiled from his own kingdom and had no army, Hanuman flared up. "Have you forgotten that Rama, when still a teenager, had killed Tataka and Subahu? Have you forgotten that a single arrow of Rama hurled the mighty Maricha miles away? Have you forgotten that Rama single-handedly killed fourteen thousand demons at Janasthana headed by Khara, Dushana, and Trishara? Wasn't it because of fear of Rama's valour that you plotted to abduct Sita while Rama was drawn away by Maricha? If you had dared to face Rama in a straight fight, you would have died on that very day." Concluding his proclamation of Rama's glories, Hanuman reiterated his warning to Ravana: "If you don't return Sita to Rama immediately, you too will meet the same fate as your cohorts at Janasthana."

What the Demoniac Attack with, They Get Attacked with

Infuriated at the impudence of a mere monkey in threatening him, Ravana ordered, "Execute this upstart!" However, Ravana's saintly brother, Vibhishana, intervened, "O Ravana, Hanuman has come as a messenger. And one of the war codes is that a messenger should never be killed." Ravana couldn't deny Vibhishana's point. But still smarting from the rebuke delivered by Hanuman, he declared, "This monkey hasn't acted like a messenger. He has vandalized our gardens and killed our warriors. He deserves to be punished. Monkeys are very proud of their tails. Let his tail be burnt."

Little did Ravana know that that very tail would soon leave a trail of devastation in his kingdom. What the ungodly do to thwart the godly, often that very thing boomerangs on them.

Acting on Ravana's command, the demons tied oiled clothes on Hanuman's tail, lit it, and started parading him through the streets once again. Meanwhile, the demonesses guarding Sita informed her about Hanuman's plight. She prayed that the fire not hurt the heroic vanara. By the potency of her prayers, the fire stopped scalding Hanuman. When he saw that the fire was still burning, but was not hurting him, he inferred that this miracle was due to Sita's prayers and thanked her in his mind. The ever-resourceful vanara recognized that his burning-but-not-hurting tail was a formidable weapon to attack the demons. Using his extraordinary powers, he broke free from his shackles and leapt on to one of Lanka's many buildings. Soon, his tail lit the building, and he jumped on to another building to similarly burn it. The demons were flabbergasted at his sudden counter-attack. By the time they regained their wits and rushed to stop him, he had already jumped to the next building. In no time, he had set nearly half of Lanka ablaze.

Hanuman exemplifies how even the destructive emotion of anger can be put to constructive use in devotional service. His anger on seeing Sita's affliction and on hearing Rama's denigration is considered righteous, for it impelled him to perform a glorious service. Nonetheless, despite his heroic channeling of the power of anger, he also demonstrates anger's inherent danger—it can make us act recklessly.

When he had set Lanka ablaze, the thought suddenly occurred to him that Sita might have been burnt in the conflagration. Horrified, he started berating himself for his impetuosity. Responding to the sincerity of his intention and the gravity of his concern, a celestial voice spoke up, assuring him that Sita was safe.

Thus reassured, Hanuman decided to complement the destruction with intimidation. Wanting to sow dissension among Lanka's citizens, he climbed atop the city's border wall. With his blazing tail creating a fearsome halo around him, he declared in a thunderous voice, "O demons, this devastation is just a prelude of what will befall Lanka unless Ravana returns Sita. I am the least powerful among Rama's servants. Countless monkeys, many more powerful than me, will soon assail Lanka. If you want to save yourselves and your city, O demons, prevail upon Ravana to return Sita."

Glancing with satisfaction at the chaos in the demons' ranks, Hanuman leapt into the air, with the victorious war-cry: "*Jay* Shri Rama." The distraught citizens of Lanka watched on mutely, petrified to see their defensive wall crumple under the pressure of his leap.

Hanuman's intrepid devotion, unflappable determination, sharp intelligence, creative resourcefulness, and ambitious service attitude—all these can inspire us in facing our battles. More importantly, his example can help us re-envision devotion as an adventure in service. While serving the Lord, if we strive to the best of our capacity, things that seem impossible will become possible. Indeed, Hanuman's glorious mission to Lanka demonstrates the concluding verse of Bhagavad-gita (18.78): for those who endeavour in harmony with the divine, ultimate victory is guaranteed.

CHAPTER SIXTEEN

Rama-Monkeys:
From the Use-and-throw Culture
to the Care-and-share Culture

In the Ramayana's climactic battle between Rama's monkey forces and Ravana's demon forces, the odds heavily favoured the demons. The monkeys had very few proper weapons, whereas the demons were armed with formidable weapons. The monkeys were on a foreign territory they had never seen before, whereas the demons were on home territory. The monkeys were far lesser organized for war than the demons. And yet the monkeys won.

Devoted to the Devoted

While the battle ultimately boils down to the final confrontation between Rama and Ravana which

Rama won decisively, the trends in the battle were set long before, with Ravana's many generals falling, one by one, to Rama's monkeys. To better appreciate the extraordinary dedication of the monkeys, let's compare the relationships of the two armies with their respective leaders.

The demons had known Ravana for a long time; he had been their monarch for decades; many of them had known him throughout their life. And despite his atrocities elsewhere while plundering and conquering the universe, he seemed to have brought phenomenal prosperity to Lanka, earning for it the sobriquet 'the golden city.' The demons had seen both Ravana's power and prosperity, with the latter being shared abundantly with his citizens.

In contrast, Rama could provide nothing to the monkeys assisting him. Having been exiled from his own kingdom, he had no wealth to share. Moreover, the monkeys hadn't known Rama for that long. For that matter, even their present king Sugriva, who was Rama's ally, hadn't been their king for that long. Yet the monkeys were ready to lay down their lives for him. Where did their dedication come from? It could partly be from the ethic of obedience to authority that is drummed deeply into soldiers. Additionally, the leading monkeys were great devotees; so, their devotion for Rama could have inspired similar devotion among the other monkeys. But beyond all such factors, the major cause of their devotion was the character of the object of their devotion: Rama.

The Ramayana brings out the contrast between Rama and Ravana graphically by describing what they did during the war at the end of each day's battles. Each night, Ravana would tell his surviving soldiers, "Throw the corpses of the slain soldiers into the ocean, and throw them in so deep, that they would not float back ashore. That way, each morning, the monkeys won't see any demons' corpses on the shore. That will dishearten them because they will think that they hadn't been able to kill any demons during their fight the previous day." Ravana spared practically no thought for his martyrs; he exhibited a literal 'use-and-throw' attitude towards them: Use them for his purposes as long as they could fight and throw them away once they couldn't fight.

In contrast, Rama, after each day's battle, stayed awake late into the night performing the last rites of his martyrs. Whereas Ravana was always above his army in his majestic chariot and his magnificent palace, Rama was always with his army, living with them, eating with them, sleeping with them, fighting with them, and grieving and praying with them on the loss of their loved ones. He cared.

During the war, every day, Rama's army saw how great a warrior he was—how he routed hordes of demons, wreaking havoc in their ranks. And every night, they saw how great a person he was, commiserating with them in their sorrows. No wonder the monkeys were ready to lay down their lives for him.

Seeking Help for Those Who Help

When the war ended with the fall of Ravana, the gods assembled in the sky, lauded Rama for his heroic achievement and urged him to ask for some benedictions. Of course, Rama, as the God of the gods, is the giver of benedictions, not the receiver. But because he had descended to the world to demonstrate the role of an ideal human being, he played that role to perfection, acting as subordinate to those who were actually subordinate to him.

Every night of the war, he prayed, "I don't need any benediction for himself. But, O gods, if you are pleased with me, I request that you grant benedictions to the monkeys who fought heroically by my side. They have accepted immense hardships for my cause. I request that they be blessed with abundant food and water wherever they lived. O immortal ones, please also revive the monkeys who had been slain but whose bodies hadn't been totally mutilated." The gods happily granted those blessings, and those monkeys sprang back to life, healthy and happy.

Soon, after Sita was reunited with Rama and Vibhishana was crowned the king of Lanka, the time came for Rama to return to Ayodhya, which meant that he would be separated from the monkeys. The separation came so suddenly as to seem like a rupture. With his fourteen-year exile nearly ending, Rama was anxious to return to Ayodhya on time—primarily because Bharata had said that he wouldn't sustain his life for one moment beyond the fourteen years.

Bharata had agreed to act as Rama's surrogate in Ayodhya, but only for the fourteen years of Rama's exile.

To ensure that he reached Ayodhya in time, Rama, on the suggestion of Vibhishana, decided to take the Pushpaka plane that Ravana had stolen from his cousin, the treasurer of the gods, Kuvera. As Rama was about to ascend the chariot and depart, he saw the solemn, even dejected, faces of the monkeys. Reading their mind, Rama invited them to join him in the plane, which had the mystical capacity to expand. And thus the monkeys had the ride of their life as they flew through the sky along with their beloved Lord to his kingdom.

When the plane was flying over Kishkinda, the monkey's kingdom, Rama ordered the plane to descend and asked the monkeys to invite their wives and children to join in the journey to Ayodhya. Thus, they all came to Rama's capital and had a wonderful time enjoying the festivities as they beheld the glorious coronation of their glorious Lord.

Rama's example demonstrates how we can be mindful of those who serve us. In today's corporate culture, where interactions tend to become highly depersonalized, where employees may be handed the pink slip on any day without even the least intimation, where security guards watch over fired employees as they clear their tables lest the disgruntled employees place some bugs in their computers or otherwise sabotage the projects from which they have been evicted, where termination is conveyed in such heavily sanitized jargon that people feel the voice at the other end comes from a mouthpiece, not a human being—in such a culture of superficial, short-lived relationships, the relationship between employer and employee in the Ramayana can be an inspiring model for deep, sustainable relationships.

Where employers have, like Rama, an ethos of caring and sharing, the relationships formed go beyond ordinary business-centred give-and-take to personal bonds that bring out the best from everyone for everyone's well-being.

Use-and-throw Culture

We live in a culture of use-and-throw; so many of us buy objects only to throw them away when they stop seeming attractive enough, even if they are still usable.

Such a use-and-throw attitude, when applied to things, has serious environmental consequences—huge swathes of land, water, and air resources are wasted in managing that which we have rejected as waste. Still, the consequence of this attitude may seem remote to us unless we are in the vicinity of the environmental degradation. However, when the use-and-throw attitude is applied to human beings, the cost is far more immediately and intensely felt. We may not feel that cost when we happen to be the holders of this attitude, but we do feel it when we become its targets—when people trash us out of their lives. We may rant at their insensitivity or even monstrosity, but their actions are simply the bitter fruits of the seeds that we have sown, individually and socially. Which seeds? The seeds of the materialistic culture we have adopted. In such a culture, life has no purpose except to enjoy material pleasures—and others' existence has no purpose unless they contribute to our material pleasure. While most of us won't verbalize things that bluntly, sanitized speech doesn't change the reality—it only dulls our awareness of the reality.

In contrast with such a materialistic worldview, a spiritual worldview is far more conducive to cultivating a culture of care and share. Within a spiritual vision, we see people not as things to be used for our gratification but as persons with emotions who, in their essential nature, are just like us. We understand that we all are souls. And all souls are parts of the Whole, who manifests in various personal manifestations such as Rama and Krishna. When we see that we all are parts of the one same divine family, we don't depersonalize others, but sense our connection with them and feel inspired to treat them more personally.

Personal interactions are best fostered by not just a spiritual worldview but by a spiritual devotional worldview. When we practice bhakti-yoga to kindle our devotion to the personal Whole, that practice infuses within us a service attitude towards him and by extension to his parts, thus foundationally transforming how we relate with others.

The One Master among Many Masters

That the Lord is the supreme master eminently worthy of our service and devotion is a recurrent theme in bhakti literature. The great saint Kulashekhara, who had been a powerful king in his pre-devotional life, compares serving the Lord with serving an ordinary master in an insightful verse from his devotional composition, Mukunda-mala-stotra (Text 17): 'Our master, the Personality of Godhead Narayana, who alone rules the three worlds, whom one can serve in meditation, and who happily shares His personal domain, is manifest before us. Yet still we beg for the service of some minor lord of a few villages, some lowly man who can only meagerly reward us. Alas, what foolish wretches we are!'

He contrasts worldly masters with the divine master on four counts:

1. **The master's position:** Materialistic masters may be owners of a few villages. The verse stated in the previous paragraph was composed at a time when feudal lords owned most of the lands; today's bosses might be characterized as being owners of a few thousand square feet of office space. In contrast with both feudal lords and corporate bosses, the Lord is the owner of all of existence. His wealth is beyond compare—in fact, he is the master of the Goddess of Fortune, who is the source of all fortune.

2. **The master's character:** Materialistic masters are often self-centred and selfish; they usually see us as factors in the production equation that is meant to fill their coffers. In contrast, the Lord is selfless and caring; he accompanies us lifetime after lifetime as our immanent friend and guide, eager to prompt us towards spiritual evolution and the supreme happiness thereof.

3. **The endeavour needed for serving:** Materialistic masters often make us slave for them till we reach our breaking point. While this characterization may not apply to all worldly bosses, the principle of exploitation is widely present in corporate culture. As is sarcastically and yet truly said, 'The harder you work, the nicer the vacation—your boss goes on.' In contrast, the Lord can be served simply by remembrance—if we just remember him affectionately, he is pleased by that expression of devotion. Of course, devotees naturally want to serve him more and more, assisting in his mission of compassion to benefit all living beings. But even if we are circumstantially unable to contribute practically, as when we become diseased or aged, the privilege of serving him is not denied to us—we can still serve him simply by cultivating his devotional remembrance and thus progress towards him.

4. **The reward for the service:** Materialistic masters offer as reward some money that we can

use to take care of our needs and maybe some of our desires. In contrast, the Lord offers us the supreme liberation—residence in his personal abode as his eternal associate. Attaining that abode frees us from unworthy yet unending bodily cravings and fulfils our deepest need—our longing to love and be loved.

The foregoing doesn't necessarily mean that we shouldn't serve our bosses—it means that we shouldn't identify ourselves with that role, but should harmonize that role with our identity as servants of our eternal Lord.

Devotion's Inclusiveness: Unqualified, but Not Disqualified

While the above four factors focus on the Lord and what he as the master brings to the bhakti table, another theme recurrent in bhakti literature is that we don't need to bring much—all we need is the desire to serve. Even if we are materially unqualified, having no significant abilities, or having a regrettable track record of wrongdoings, we are still never disqualified.

Rama, by engaging monkeys in his service, demonstrates that his service is open to everyone. He doesn't need us to be highly trained and qualified to be able to serve him. We can start our service from where we are with what we have. And he, by his inconceivable potency, will guide and empower us to do more and better service.

Of course, many of the monkeys serving Rama were gods who had descended from the celestial realm to the terrestrial realm through the path of monkey wombs. Still, the fact that those gods took birth in the humble monkey species and from there rendered extraordinary service is instructive and illustrative of the inclusiveness of bhakti.

Thus, the Ramayana gives us the confidence that no matter how unqualified we may be, we are never disqualified—we can still strive to serve our Lord and thereby progress devotionally towards inner satisfaction and outer contribution.

When we learn to live in harmony with our nature as the servants of our Lord, we become conscious agents of change who help replace the use-and-throw culture with the care-and-share culture.

CHAPTER SEVENTEEN

Vibhishana-Ravana:
Betrayer or Benefactor?

Life sometimes presents us moments when we have to make colossal choices. While every choice has consequences, some choices are far more consequential than others. What we choose at critical moments defines what we become.

The Ramayana depicts one such moment in the life of Vibhishana, the virtuous younger brother of the vicious demon, Ravana.

Transcendental Concern, Practical Counsel

After the fire set in Lanka by Hanuman had been doused, Ravana summoned his assembly.

Praising his generals for having ably assisted him in his conquests all over the universe, he said that he now depended on them to form a plan for dealing with Rama's impending invasion.

On hearing his words, several of Ravana's generals hastened to assure him that they had nothing to fear from anyone. Hanuman had caused some damage because he had caught them unawares. But now they would be prepared and could easily crush any ragtag army of humans and monkeys.

The only dissenter was Ravana's youngest brother, Vibhishana. Though sharing his brother's blood, he did not share his demoniac disposition. When the three brothers, Ravana, Kumbhakarna, and Vibhishana, had performed austerities to appease the gods, Ravana and Kumbhakarna had contrived to ask for immortality, but Vibhishana had asked simply for constant remembrance of the immortal Lord.

While living in Lanka, he had pursued his own devotion without interfering with Ravana's schemes. He knew that Ravana was unlikely to listen to him. And he didn't have the might to stop Ravana by force. But now when Ravana had abducted Sita, his Lord's consort, Vibhishana found the atrocity intolerable. Yet he knew that revealing his devotional agony would alienate him from the demons, ruining whatever chance he had of getting Sita released without a war. So, he spoke in a language intelligible to the Rakshasas—the language of military might.

Addressing Ravana, Vibhishana stood and spoke, "O

king of the demons, you have conquered the universe on the strength of boons that make you invulnerable to the gods. But the invulnerability granted by those boons doesn't extend to our present opponents—humans and monkeys." Ordinarily, humans and monkeys were .no threat to demons, who were much more powerful. So, Ravana had scornfully neglected asking for protection from them.

Continuing his cautionary counsel, Vibhishana said, "Our present antagonists are not ordinary. The human and the monkey both have exhibited awesome power. Rama had single-handedly overpowered at Janasthana an entire army comprising fourteen thousand formidable demons. And Hanuman had single-handedly penetrated the impregnable-seeming Lanka, killed several of our prominent generals, burned nearly half of the kingdom, and escaped unharmed. If an army made of such humans and monkeys were to attack Lanka, we can scarcely imagine the devastation they may wreck. Please, O Ravana, return Sita to Rama, and save Lanka from a devastating war."

Though Ravana found Vibhishana's well-reasoned words unpalatable, still they made him circumspect. He announced to the assembly, "Let us adjourn till the next day; I need time to think about the issue overnight."

Unsated Lust and Unfettered Arrogance

The next morning at dawn, Vibhishana went to meet Ravana in his palace. The demon-king greeted his brother, but his disposition had changed. Where he had seemed pensive the previous evening, now he seemed impervious to good counsel. A night of unsated craving for Sita had eroded Ravana's intelligence. Despairing, Vibhishana tried an additional line of argument. "O Ravana, I have noticed—and surely you too must have noticed—that a series of ill omens have started appearing in Lanka. And they all started since Sita has been brought here." Though Ravana heard Vibhishna's words, they couldn't enter his head, which was filled with a combination of unfulfilled lust and unfettered arrogance. Declaring that he would never give up Sita, he contemptuously derided Rama and turned away from Vibhishana.

That day, Ravana summoned a full council of war. After all his warriors had assembled, he declared his intent to wage war for keeping Sita. But he encountered criticism from an unexpected quarter. The colossal Kumbhakarna, Ravana's younger brother, chastised him, "O brother, you are consulting us now, but why did you not consult us before abducting Sita? It is because of your rashness that we are all in grave danger." But he ended on a note that was supportive, though self-congratulatory: "Still, you needn't worry; you are fortunate to have a brother like me who can destroy any army and undo whatever damage you have done." Though smarting at being publically admonished, Ravana controlled himself and thanked his brother for his support—the giant demon was too valuable an ally to alienate.

Although dissuading Ravana from his obstinacy seemed to be a lost cause, Vibhishana resolved to keep trying till the end. He presented sound arguments, but they fell not just on deaf ears but also on angry minds. Several demons interrupted and chided Vibhishana throughout his speech. After Vibhishana finished, Ravana's son, Indrajita, reviled his uncle. "It is the misfortune of the demons that we have among us a coward who has more regard for our opponents' might than our own. The motley army of humans and monkeys that you speak so highly of—just one of the great demons here will be enough to annihilate that army."

Vibhishana recognized that Indrajita was a major source of Ravana's false confidence. Adopting a do-or-die attitude, he tried to expose the prince's bluff and bravado. "O prince, your words arise only from your willful ignorance of our opponents' might. Fighting against them is to court self-destruction. Anyone who recommends such a war to a king is actually the king's enemy."

However, the bond between father and son, sealed by their shared arrogance, was too thick to be cut, even when the cutting sword was made of truthful words. Outraged at the insinuation that his son was acting as his enemy, Ravana blasted Vibhishana. "No matter how well a king takes care of his relatives, some of them still remain ingrates. They hunger for power, create dissensions among their own people, and work against those who have always done them good. They are the actual enemies of the king and the kingdom."

Making a last-ditch effort, Vibhishana reminded Ravana, "Sycophants who second one's words can be found by the dozens, but real friends who speak the truth, even when it is unpalatable, are rare." The irony implicit in Vibhishana's words was not lost to the assembly. At the start of the council meeting, Ravana had said, "O ministers, with your help, I have conquered the universe. A king who acts on his own whims is foolish, whereas a king who takes counsel from his ministers is wise." Ravana's own words had now come back to bite him. Snorting derisively, he turned away from Vibhishana.

Summoning all the humility at his command, Vibhishana implored Ravana, "Do not take the whole race of demons on a course of self-destruction." To emphasize that his counsel was not motivated by any hunger for power, Vibhishana placed his own crown at Ravana's feet, symbolizing thereby that he was ready to renounce his royal opulence. For an honourable kshatriya hero to thus demean himself was astonishing.

But it was all in vain. Ravana kicked away Vibhishana's crown. And Indrajita reviled him with even harsher words.

Betraying the Betrayer Is Not Betrayal

Being rejected and reviled, Vibhishana left the court and left Ravana. Some people hold that by joining Rama's side, Vibhishana betrayed his brother, but actually his brother had betrayed their clan. Vibhishana simply did what it took to minimize the harm caused to his clan by that betrayal.

A king is meant to protect people, especially five classes of people—the elderly, the saintly, the cows, the children, and the women. Ravana had already done exactly the opposite of his duty by abducting Sita. But now he was doing something much more irresponsible. By stubbornly holding on to Sita despite knowing that it would plunge the whole of Lanka into a destructive war, he was leading to doom all those whom he was meant to protect. Being blinded by lust for Sita, he was betraying his whole clan. Therefore, Vibhishana decided that his duty to his clan was higher than his duty to the present leader of that clan.

Vibhishana had three options ahead of him. First, he could attempt an internal coup in Lanka, overthrow Ravana, and return Sita to Rama, thereby avoiding the war. But Vibhishana knew that he wouldn't get enough support to stage a coup successfully. Most of the demons being enamoured by Ravana's strength would underestimate the danger from Rama's invasion. Or being scared of Ravana's strength, they wouldn't dare to rebel against him.

Second, Vibhishana could just renounce everything material and leave the messy world of politics far behind. But such renunciation would be a dereliction of duty; as a member of the royal family, he had a duty to do whatever he could to protect the citizens. By renouncing the world, he would be failing in that duty—during and after the war, Lanka's citizens would be slaughtered.

Third, he could go over to Rama's side and convey to him that Ravana's abduction of Sita was not supported by all the Rakshasas. Further, by helping Rama to rescue Sita, he could, on behalf of the Rakshasa clan, do his part in countering Ravana's misdeed.

Of course, Vibhishana's topmost consideration was how he could best serve his worshipable Lord Rama. His devotion was the essence of who he was. He had tried to the best of his capacity to be faithful to his brother while simultaneously being true to his devotional principles. But now when his brother was bent on antagonizing Rama, Vibhishana knew that by being faithful to such a person, he would be betraying himself.

Finite Submission, Infinite Protection

Vibhishana's siding with Rama was an act of incredible courage. Normally, in a conflict when a person defects from one side to another, the defector usually seeks and secures a guarantee of safety from the side to which he is defecting. Without such a guarantee, the defector risks the wretched fate of being trapped in no man's land. The side from which he has defected treats him as a traitor to be punished ruthlessly—and the bloodthirsty cannibal

Rakshasas specialized in such ruthlessness. And the side to which he defects also views him suspiciously, as a possible spy or at least as a newcomer whose loyalty is suspect.

Expectedly, when Vibhishana came over to Rama's camp across the ocean, the monkeys were skeptical. Hanuman alone recognized Vibhishana's non-duplicitousness. Rama accepted Hanuman's recommendation that Vibhishana be welcomed. Reciprocating with the demon's courageous surrender, Rama embraced him. He proclaimed, "I guarantee eternal protection to those who surrender to me, even if they express their surrender only once." This verse is declared by the great saint and scholar Srila Ramanujacharya to be one of the *carama-shlokas* (ultimate verses) of the bhakti tradition. Stressing the universality of his protection, Rama further declared that he would grant protection to even Ravana if he surrendered.

Once the alliance of Rama and Vibhishana was sealed, Rama had Vibhishana crowned as the king of Lanka even though the current king of Lanka was still alive. Through this coronation, Rama conveyed his confidence that he would surely win the war. More importantly for Vibhishana, Rama conveyed that he had no intention of destroying all of Lanka; he intended to destroy only its despotic ruler. And he also conveyed that he had no intention of annexing Lanka either; he intended to restore it to a more responsible demon ruler.

Vibhishana proved in every way to be worthy of the faith that Rama reposed in him. He helped Rama's monkeys identify spies that Ravana had sent into their ranks and guided them to see through the wicked tricks of the demons, thereby playing a pivotal role in their ultimate victory.

Devotion Harmonizes the Material and the Spiritual

Vibhishana's choosing Rama can be seen as a rejection of the material for the spiritual—he renounced his bodily relationships for his devotional relationship with Rama. Though correct, this perspective is incomplete.

The highest, most informed spiritual level is the devotional level. Bhakti philosophy explains that we don't need to always renounce the material for the spiritual because the spiritual and the material are not necessarily opposite—both come from the supreme, and both are meant to be used in the service of their source.

In fact, the specialty of bhakti-yoga among the various yogic paths is·that it doesn't require the rejection of the material for the spiritual; it facilitates the harmonization of both the material and the spiritual with the Supreme.

Pertinently however, everything material is not equal in its spiritual adaptability. Within the material, some things may be pro-spiritual; some, non-spiritual; some, anti-spiritual. We need to reject the anti-spiritual material, regulate the non-spiritual material, and channelize the pro-spiritual material.

Vibhishana rejected his anti-spiritual material relationships with Ravana and his cohorts. He channeled his pro-spiritual material relationships—four of his associates joined him in surrendering to Rama. Through it all, he acted as the benefactor of everyone.

The Bhagavad-gita (05.29) states that God is the benefactor of all living beings, and later (12.13) states that those devoted to God are also the benefactors of all living beings. The best thing we can do for anyone is inspire them to connect with God, the source of all auspiciousness, and caution them about *adharma* that alienates them from God and sentences them to grievous karmic reactions. Vibhishana always desired the best for Ravana. Unfortunately, the demon-king, due to his lust and arrogance, remained blind to his own good and mistook his well-wishers to be enemies.

Though Ravana never saw Vibhishana as his benefactor, Lanka's citizens saw Vibhishana as such after the war. They said that the defeat of their kingdom didn't end in plunder and mayhem, but led only to the smooth transfer of power to a capable king of their own dynasty, who ruled them fairly and wisely.

Perhaps the most important lesson from Vibhishana's story is that we are defined not by where we come from, but by where we choose to go. Though Vibhishana came from a demoniac family, he chose to go to the side of virtue. And thus he is famed not as a demon, but as a devotee—his demoniac background underscores bhakti's potency for redeeming everyone and highlights his glory in courageously choosing God.

Irrespective of where we have come from, the path to choose the Lord remains open for us at every moment. Our choice may not seem as dramatic as was Vibhishana's. Still every ordinary moment in which we choose the Lord, we strengthen our moral and spiritual muscles. Those muscles will empower us to choose wisely during the momentous moments of life-defining choices.

CHAPTER EIGHTEEN

Rama-Ravana:
Lust Bites the Dust

The Ramayana culminates in a massive war between the vicious Ravana and the virtuous Rama. The confrontation between them is triggered by Ravana's abduction of Rama's wife, Sita. But its seeds were sowed much earlier, by the demon's atrocities that had extended for a long time.

Ravana is traditionally seen as the embodiment of lust. Herein, embodiment refers not to the fictional concretization of a human attribute, but to a paradigmatic individual in whom that attribute is strikingly manifested.

Ravana's Rampage Repelled

As the war neared its finale, all of Ravana's foremost warriors had been dispatched by him to the battlefield and dispatched by Rama's forces from the battlefield and the world.

Realizing that the fate of the war now depended on him alone, Ravana came out to fight with the last of his forces. He fought furiously, tearing through the ranks of the vanaras trying to reverse the odds that he had thought were overwhelmingly in his favour at the start of the war, but were now overwhelmingly against him. His initial derisive dismissal—"What can a motley band of humans and monkeys do?"—had changed to disbelieving despair: "What have these humans and monkeys done?"

Unable to tolerate the thought of his defeat or demise, Ravana fought remorselessly, felling opponents wherever he went. Seeing him devastating the vanaras, Rama confronted him. The two great warriors fought intensely. Despite his many boons, Ravana just couldn't match Rama's speed and skill in archery. Slowly but unstoppably, he started losing ground. One by one, his bow was cut, his charioteer killed, his chariot wrecked, and his armour destroyed. He was rendered weaponless, defenseless, motionless—an easy target for Rama's final fatal arrows.

But Rama graciously spared the demon. He desired victory through a fair fight between the two of them at their best. As Ravana had already fought many great vanara warriors on that day, he would now be tired. Telling Ravana to retreat, rest, and return the next day, Rama let him go.

Though spared, Ravana felt humiliated. Yet he had no alternative except to turn and run back to his palace while Rama still remained benevolently disposed.

The Final Battle

The next morning, Ravana marched out of Lanka, determined to avenge his humiliation. Soon, both Ravana and Rama, who had been fighting other opponents, came face-to-face. Just as their fight was about to begin, a magnificent chariot descended in front of Rama. The charioteer bowed to Rama and explained that Indra had sent his chariot and charioteer to assist Rama, who had till then been fighting from Hanuman's shoulder.

The arrival of a celestial chariot was another reminder to Ravana that he wasn't fighting an ordinary human being. Of course, had he been in a mood to learn, he could have already learnt that lesson by seeing how Rama had felled his colossal and near-invincible brother, Kumbhakarna, and how Rama's warriors had felled all his foremost warriors who had bested even the gods. In fact, he could have learnt that lesson even before the war had begun. How? By contemplating Rama's feat of single-handedly overpowering the fourteen thousand demons Ravana had stationed at his outpost in Janasthana. Such a feat was far beyond the ken of any human being. Yet the same obstinacy that had blinded Ravana lifelong kept him blind when death stared him in the face.

Incensed to see Indra helping his opponent, Ravana launched a ferocious attack. After a fearsome battle that left both warriors bloodied, Rama slowly gained the upper hand with his peerless archery. Overwhelming Ravana with his unrelenting fusillade of arrows, Rama used divine arrows to cut off the demon's heads. To his consternation, however, those heads soon reappeared. He cut them off again, and they appeared again.

Seeing Rama perplexed, Ravana laughed malevolently, convinced of his invulnerability. With blinding speed, he redoubled his attack, trying to turn the tables on Rama. Ravana had got benedictions from the gods that if his heads or limbs were cut off, they would reappear. He had frequently used that benediction to baffle his opponents and then overpower them. That was how he had overcome the aged vulture Jatayu who had become exhausted after the stupendous effort of ripping off several of Ravana's heads and arms.

But unlike the aged Jatayu, Rama was young. And he had another crucial advantage—an ally who knew Ravana's weakness. The demon's younger brother, Vibhishana, had gone over to Rama's side, being appalled by Ravana's remorseless viciousness.

On seeing Rama stymied by Ravana's seeming invincibility, Vibhishana rushed to Rama's side and informed him that Ravana's life-force was kept hidden in his heart. Destroying that life-force by attacking his heart was the only way to fell the wicked demon.

Inferring that his secret was being revealed, Ravana

rebuked Vibhishana and increased the ferocity of his attack on Rama. Wanting to finish the demon, Rama uttered a mantra given by the sage Agastya, known as the Aditya Hridaya. That mantra's mystic energy rejuvenated and empowered him. Invoking one of most powerful celestial arrows at his command, he aimed it at Ravana's heart and fired it with breathtaking speed. Despite the demon's frantic efforts to ward off that missile, it unrelentingly pierced his heart. With a howl that shook the earth, the demon fell, never to rise again.

Significance of Ravana's Reappearing Heads

The Ramayana is *Itihasa*, a genre of spiritual literature that is based on historical accounts. Yet its significance extends far beyond mere historical reporting. It depicts timeless values that can guide people through all times in history to attain the world beyond history—to the timeless spiritual arena of existence.

Seen from such a value-centred perspective, Ravana's reappearing heads might be seen as representing our lower desires. Even if we reject one such desire, others keep appearing, as did Ravana's heads. Just as Rama succeeded only when he directed his arrow not towards the heads, but towards the heart, similarly, we can succeed when we direct our purificatory effort not towards specific desires but towards our heart, towards the misdirection of our love away from the Lord to the world.

Ravana's ten heads were conspicuous. Yet his strength lay not there, but in a less conspicuous part—his heart. Similarly, gross wrongdoings are conspicuous. But what corrupts us most is not such specific wrongdoings, but our fundamental wrongdoing of being disconnected from divinity. Wrongdoing refers not just to the wrong we do, but also the right we don't do. As long as we don't do the right of connecting devotionally with our Lord, we will keep succumbing to one wrong desire or another—the heads will keep reappearing. When we make our heart right by practising bhakti-yoga diligently, our lower desires gradually get exiled from our heart, fully and forever.

The fall of Ravana is commemorated in the festival of Dussehra wherein huge effigies of the demon-king are set ablaze. Often, a flaming arrow is shot at the wooden effigies, re-enacting Rama's fatal attack on Ravana. Just as Ravana's fall was celebrated with cheers by the many gods and sages assembled to watch the battle, so too is the fall of Ravana's effigies cheered by onlookers assembled for Dussehra.

The imagery centred on fire is significant. Fire sacrifices are time-honoured means for sanctification. Additionally, fire is used for cremation after death. The body's cremation releases the soul from any lingering attachment to its physical shell, freeing it to travel to its next destination.

The incineration of Ravana's effigies can be said to signify the incineration of our lower desires and the sanctification of our consciousness, which becomes detached and free to rise to higher levels of reality. While cheering the razing of Ravana's effigy, we can pray that our lower desires be similarly razed by the purifying fire of devotion.

Gender Depictions

Some people feel that Indian traditions portray women negatively as agents of illusion, for they represent the illusory energy, Maya, who too is personified as a female. However, the foremost force of illusion is lust, and it is embodied as Ravana, a male.

Philosophically speaking, lust in particular and illusion in general are gender-neutral. The same Ramayana that depicts the masculine Ravana as an embodiment of lust also depicts his sister, Shurapanakha, as a female embodiment of lust. In fact, it was her lust for Rama and her subsequent assault on Sita, whom she saw as her competitor in gaining Rama's attention, that escalated tensions between Rama and Ravana. Worse still, when Ravana had become circumspect on learning of Rama's formidable power, it was Shurapanakha who inflamed his lusty imagination by fueling it with provocative descriptions of Sita's beauty.

Bhagavad-gita section (03.36-43) that analyzes lust—how it deludes and how it can be defeated—doesn't use any gender-specific language or imagery. To the contrary, the Gita (03.40) states that lust is present in all living beings—in their senses, mind, and intelligence. Lust deludes and degrades everyone it controls; it makes men into monsters and women into witches. Captivated by lust, men perpetrate barbaric atrocities to gratify their desires, and women bewitch and befool others with their feminine charms.

In contemporary culture, sexual violence is often strongly condemned, and rightly so. Ironically however, the same culture also depicts explicit images, and rationalizes such depiction as the right to free expression. In a culture that features both moral perversity and moral ambiguity, the Ramayana's gender-neutral narrative of the universal consequences of uncontrolled lust sounds an essential cautionary note.

DUST Acronym

The phrase 'bite the dust' signifies defeat, often an ignominious defeat. This usage derives from sports such as wrestling wherein the winner holds the loser down, metaphorically making the latter bite the dust. It could be said that Rama's fatal arrow made Ravana bite the dust. His fall represents the fate of those who give themselves to lust.

Additionally, dust in a devotional context refers to the sacred dust of the lotus feet of the Lord and of those devoted to him. Such dust is considered immensely pure, capable of purging us of our worldly desires. Indeed, becoming blessed by sacred dust is considered an essential purpose of practising bhakti-yoga.

And how that process of bhakti-yoga can help us overcome lust can be explicated using the acronym DUST—Determination, Understanding, Submission, Training.

Determination: Suppose we are infected with a lethal but curable disease. When the gravity of the disease registers within us, we become determined to take the treatment, even if it is demanding. Similarly, when the grave consequences of infection by lust register within us, we must muster determination to curb and cure it, even if doing so is difficult. The Gita (02.41) underscores the need for single-pointed determination. We may have resolved to curb our lower desires in the past and failed. Such failures may dishearten us into thinking that we just don't have the necessary determination.

However, we all have determination; it's just misdirected. Take people's addiction to alcohol, for example. They may complain that they lack determination to give it up, but, they *do* have determination—only the drive is misdirected towards consuming copious amounts of alcohol, even if it leads to distressing consequences. In our conditioned stage, we use our determination to gratify our lower desires. We need to redirect that same determination in the opposite direction—to fight those desires.

Understanding: Gita wisdom helps us understand the deceptive nature of licentious desires—they promise huge pleasure, but deliver only meagre pleasure, which too soon gives way to massive trouble. More importantly, bhakti literatures help us understand where lust comes from. Love for the Lord is central to our spiritual nature. When it becomes misdirected to worldly objects, it transmogrifies into lust. And when lust is indulged in indiscriminately, it becomes insatiable.

When we lead a life of dharma and practice bhakti-yoga for redirecting our love to the Lord, our desires become slowly but surely purified.

This understanding of how lust originates and how it can be redirected complements our determination.

Submission: Our fundamental malaise is the desire to seek pleasure separate from God, whose name Rama conveys that he is the reservoir of all pleasure. The Gita (15.07) states that we are eternal parts of the Lord; when we act apart from him, we end up enticed and enslaved by the lower desires in our mind and senses. If we want to end our subordination to our lowers desires, we need to cultivate submission to our Lord.

Lest the notion of submission cause some visceral aversion, it's important to stress that devotional submission to the Lord is not at all like worldly submission. Whereas worldly submission is sometimes demeaning, submission to the One who is our greatest benefactor is uplifting and empowering. This submission is out of love, just as those in love may say to their beloved, "Your wish is my command." When we submit ourselves to the Lord, his omnipotence empowers us to overpower our lower desires. By our diligent practice of bhakti-yoga, devotional submission blossoms into devotional absorption, and we transcend our lower desires.

Training: Just as a patient who has been immobilized needs training to walk again, we are spiritually immobilized, being afflicted by our lower desires which ground our consciousness at the material level. We need training to walk spiritually, that is, to raise our consciousness to the spiritual level. Bhakti-yoga offers this training. Devotional processes—such as chanting the holy names, studying scriptures, and associating with spiritual people—train us, through both precept and example, to keep our consciousness spiritual even amidst life's temptations and tribulations. The more we practise bhakti-yoga, the more we become trained to keep our consciousness safe and spiritual. We learn to purposefully focus our consciousness on the constructive things we need to do, instead of letting our lower desires drag it to our default attachments.

When lust is thus treated with dust, what results is liberation—liberation both in this world and beyond it too. Liberation from shortsighted desires during our stay in this world, and eventually liberation from this material world itself to our Lord's eternal abode for a life of unending pure love.

CHAPTER NINETEEN

Victimizer or Sacrificer? Four Reflections on Rama's Abandoning Sita

Rama's forsaking Sita is the Ramayana's most challenged and most challenging incident. A man's abandoning his pregnant wife because of an unproven accusation seems troublingly wrong. Let's analyze this using the acronym SEES—Sacrifice, Ethical Dilemma, Esoteric Explanations, and Selflessness.

Sacrifice

It is sometimes thought that Rama exiled Sita because he was excessively reputation-conscious. Did he abandon Sita just because he didn't want his good name sullied by having a wife suspected to be impure? But if he had been so obsessed with his reputation, then why did he not remarry after sending Sita away? A king overly concerned about appearances would want a trophy queen by his side; being a queen-less king was hardly a reputation enhancer.

As a wealthy, powerful emperor, Rama could have married anyone of his choice. But he refused to remarry because he wanted to honour his word to Sita. Soon after their marriage, Rama had promised Sita that she would be his only wife. By keeping that pledge lifelong, Rama showed his respect for Sita, thereby rebutting her accusers.

If Rama had wanted to remarry, he could have justified giving up that pledge on the grounds of religious duty. As a king, he was expected to perform sacrifices meant for his state's welfare. And tradition mandated that the sponsor perform such sacrifices with his wife. When priests pointed out this requirement and exhorted Rama to remarry, he respectfully but firmly refused. He honoured the traditional requirement by making a golden image of Sita and seating it beside him during the sacrifices. By according this honour to her through her image, he proclaimed that he still considered her his wife. And that he still considered her pure, so pure in fact that her image could sit next to him in rituals that often required exacting standards of purity.

Ethical Dilemma

If Rama considered Sita pure, why did he abandon her? Because the ethical dilemma confronting him didn't seem amenable to any other solution.

We need to see the actions of characters in the epics in the light of the prevailing culture and its cherished values. The Ramayana depicts a deeply spiritual culture. Therein, people saw success not just in terms of prosperity in this world, but also in terms of the spirituality cultivated during one's journey through this world. Cultivating spirituality, in its highest sense, meant developing devotion to the source of everything, God, and harmonizing one's whole life accordingly. In such a culture, all relations and positions were seen as opportunities for sacred service, service to God and to others in relationship with him. One service was the service of exemplifying detachment, especially from things that came in the way of one's spiritual growth.

Most people are attached materially to their relations and positions. Such attachments can keep them alienated from God, who is the ultimate provider of everything, including family members, and who is the ultimate shelter after death, when all family members are left behind. Materially attached people are naturally attracted to those with lavish material assets. The person with the most impressive material assets is usually the king. If the king demonstrates detachment by not letting material things come in the way of spiritual cultivation, then the king's example forcefully edifies citizens about the importance of life's spiritual side. So, integral to the king's duty was the duty of demonstrating to his citizens that worldly attachments couldn't sway him from his spiritual dharma. This duty conflicted with Rama's duty as a husband.

When Rama heard the accusation leveled against Sita, he was faced with an ethical dilemma. Whereas a moral dilemma confronts us with two choices, one moral and the other immoral, an ethical dilemma confronts us with two choices, both moral. For resolving an ethical dilemma, we need to discern the higher moral principle and harmonize the lower moral principle as much as possible. Rama's dilemma was ethical because his duty as a king conflicted with his duty as a husband.

As a husband, he was duty-bound to protect his wife. But as the king, he was duty-bound to exemplify and teach detachment to his citizens. If his citizens felt that he was so attached to Sita as to keep her despite her impurity, then they would, consciously or subconsciously, use Rama's alleged attachment to rationalize their own attachments to unworthy things.

Of course, Sita was not impure. She had not left Rama and gone to Ravana; Ravana had abducted her against her will. Ravana hadn't forcibly violated her because he had been cursed to die if he ever violated a woman against her will. He had tried to gain Sita's consent by alternately tempting and threatening her. She had heroically preserved her purity by spurning his temptations and braving his threats for an endlessly long year.

Rama himself had no doubts about Sita's purity. But

anticipating people's objections, he had prepared to address them. After the fall of Ravana in Lanka, when Sita was brought into his presence, he had her purity dramatically demonstrated through a test of fire. Sita entered into a fire and emerged unscathed by dint of her chastity. Moreover, after that test, the gods led by Brahma had certified Sita's spotless character.

Despite all this vindication of Sita's purity, if people were still questioning, Rama felt that nothing would ever convince them. If he neglected such people and continued to live with Sita, it would appear that he was attached to her. If he silenced them, he would come off as so blinded by attachment as to be vindictive. He felt that his duty as a king required him to show his detachment from Sita.

Exhibiting a stoic spirit of sacrifice, Rama deemed his duty as king more important than his duty as husband, and so sent Sita away to the forest. But he didn't entirely neglect his duty as a husband; he did that duty too because the forsaken Sita was still in his kingdom and thus, indirectly, in his protection.

When the distraught Lakshmana informed Sita of Rama's decision, she was devastated. But soon she regained her composure, understood her Lord's heart, and gracefully accepted her part in the heart-wrenching sacrifice that both of them had to be part of. She didn't resent Rama and didn't poison her sons against their father. She raised them lovingly, accepting with fortitude the role of a single mother that had been thrust on her.

Of course, she was not a single mother in the modern

sense; she didn't have to single-handedly earn a living and care for her children. After being forsaken, she lived in Valmiki's hermitage, where the matronly female hermits took care of her and helped her to take care of her children.

It's worth noting that banishment may not be the best word for describing Sita's abandonment. Banishment implied being evicted from the kingdom into the forest—as had happened to Rama earlier in the Ramayana. Though Sita lived in the forest, she was still in Rama's kingdom. She did not have to scour for food, clothing, or shelter; these were arranged for in Valmiki's hermitage.

Esoteric Explanations

For those seeking explanations for Sita's banishment based on past-life causes, the Valmiki Ramayana offers one and the broader Rama tradition offers many. The epic (6.51.15) mentions an ancient curse that ordained the separation of Vishnu and Lakshmi. Once, when the demons were fleeing from the gods led by Indra, they took shelter of the sage Bhrugu's wife, Khyati. When the gods asked that the demons be handed over to them so that they could be duly punished, Khyati became incited by a misguided sense of compassion. Summoning her mystic powers, she started attacking the gods, who beseeched Vishnu for help. A hard-earned win against deadly demons was being undone because of Khyati's misplaced protectiveness. To prevent such a catastrophe, Vishnu was constrained to use his own mystical disc, *Sudarshan* Chakra, for slaying her. When Bhrugu came to know about this, he became enraged. He cursed Vishnu to take multiple births in the material world and, in one such birth, to be separated from his wife—just as Bhrugu was now separated from his.

Of course, Rama as the Supreme Being is not subject to anyone's curse. Still, he accepted it out of deference to the sage and for furthering his own purpose. The enactment of that curse comprised the chain of events that led to the separation of Rama and Sita, who were Vishnu and Lakshmi incarnated on earth.

The Gaudiya Vaishnava tradition, a medieval bhakti tradition with adherents all over the world, explains that the separation of the divine couple facilitates *viraha-bhakti*, devotion in separation. Separation intensifies the devotee's remembrance of the Lord. And as the Lord is not a finite person, but is the Supreme Person, he is always present in the devotee's heart. When the devotee remembers him intensely, he reciprocates by increasingly manifesting himself in the devotee's heart, thereby intensifying the devotional trance. Externally such separation seems like agony, but internally it is the summit of spiritual ecstasy. Separation does to love what wind does to fire—spreads it more and more. When separated from Rama, Sita relished such intense devotion.

Spirit of Selflessness

The whole Ramayana is permeated with the spirit of selflessness—a spirit that attains its summit in the separation of Rama and Sita. The mood throughout the epic is not of demanding one's rights, but of selflessly sacrificing one's rights for a higher cause.

When Rama was exiled because of the promise of his father Dasharatha, Rama didn't demand his rights as the rightful heir. He could have argued: "I am utterly blameless, yet I am being not only disinherited but also exiled, as if I were the worst of criminals. And all this just for honouring some undocumented promise made by my father to my stepmother. How unfair!" Far from arguing thus, Rama immediately agreed to give up his right for the higher cause of honouring his father's words. He even calmed those who wanted to rebel against the king.

On hearing about Rama's exile, Sita too didn't fight for her rights. She didn't claim that she as a princess deserved to live in royal comforts. She willingly, even insistently, gave up those comforts for accompanying her husband to the forest.

This spirit of selflessness is illustrated by Lakshmana too when he accompanied Rama to the forest. Sita being Rama's wife was expected to stick by his side through thick and thin. But nothing of that magnitude was expected from Rama's brother. Yet Lakshmana didn't demand his right to royal comfort; instead, he gave up that comfort for the cause of serving Rama.

Bharata too demonstrated this spirit of selflessness. He could have ascended the throne, justifying that it had come of its own accord; he himself had done nothing wrong to get it. Yet, he didn't. Even when Rama entrusted the kingdom to him, he didn't consider royal luxury as his right. Though he discharged the responsibilities of a ruler, he placed Rama's sandals on the throne and sat at their feet. Emulating his brother's hermit lifestyle, he lived in a cottage outside Ayodhya and ate austere fare.

Importantly, none of these characters saw themselves as helpless victims deprived of their rights; they saw themselves as conscious agents who chose to give up their rights for a higher cause. In that same spirit, Sita, on being forsaken, didn't see herself as a victim of a judgmental husband. Recognizing that she had been called to bear a particularly heavy cross, she gracefully, even gallantly, accepted the necessary sacrifice. Those who portray her as a victim do grave injustice to her awesome strength of character.

Such people err even more if they portray Rama as a victimizer. In this incident, his position is similar to that of Sita—both are partners in an excruciating sacrifice. Perhaps the best parallel to appreciate Rama's agony in sending Sita away is Dasharatha's agony in sending Rama away.

Just as Dasharatha wanted with all his heart to offer the best of everything to his son, Rama too wanted to do everything he could for his wife. After all, she had endured, for his sake, thirteen years of austere life as a hermit and one year of agonizing life as an abductee. Just as Dasharatha was bound by duty to do something that broke his heart, so too was Rama bound by duty. At least, Dasharatha could point the finger at Kaikeyi and could vent his anger at her machinations. Rama couldn't do even that, for people would have thought him vindictive. So, he had to not only give the wrenching order of exiling Sita, but also keep the storm of his anger and agony contained within himself.

Just as Dasharatha was not punishing Rama, Rama too was not punishing Sita. Just as father and son had to make a painful sacrifice for a higher cause, husband and wife too had to make an anguishing sacrifice for a higher cause.

Injustice towards Women?

Some people see this incident as representing Indian culture's repressive attitude towards women. But is Rama's forsaking Sita meant to be a benchmark for judging all women based on unfounded suspicions? Not at all. The incident is meant primarily to illustrate the mood of sacrifice. Its specific details aren't meant to be universalized, as is evident from Rama's conduct in other situations.

That very Ramayana which describes Rama's abandoning Sita also describes Rama's mercifulness towards everyone, including women, even women looked down upon by mainstream society. The sage Gautama's wife had been literally petrified, turned into stone, because of a curse triggered by her accidental unchastity.

Rama, far from being judgmental towards her, mercifully released her from that curse and reinstated her in the respectable position of the sage's wife. The female hermit, Shabari, was treated as an outcaste, but Rama graced her by accepting the berries she offered. Tara had become widowed after the demise of her husband Vali, but Rama ensured that she was given a place of dignity in the Kishkinda palace. Considering the cultural conservatism of those times, Rama's actions were exceptionally inclusive and magnanimous.

The bhakti tradition explains that the same Absolute Truth who manifested as Rama manifested later as Krishna. And Krishna demonstrated an even more inclusive attitude towards women deemed fallen by society. Once, when he killed the demon named Bhaumasura, he came across the many princesses who had been abducted by that demon. In the prevailing conservative society, these princesses had become permanently stigmatized, even though the demon hadn't violated them. Driven by a peculiar idea of gaining religious merit, he had been waiting for an auspicious day to take the princesses for himself. Still, because these princesses had lived in the demon's captivity, society considered them defiled.

They thanked Krishna for having rescued them from the demon and begged him to rescue them from their destitute condition too. When he asked them what exactly they wanted, they requested that he accept them as his maidservants. He more than consented, making them not his maidservants, but his queens. He not only reinstated them, but also elevated them to the status of royalty in a phenomenally powerful kingdom.

Consider the contrast between the Lord's dealing with Sita and these princesses.

1. He asked Sita to pass a test by fire, but he didn't ask these princesses to undergo any such test.
2. Sita was already his queen, yet he sent her away. These princesses were unrelated to him, yet he made them his queens.
3. Sita was already pregnant with his children, so he had a major obligation to her. He had no such obligation to the princesses, yet he accepted an obligation to them and reinstated them to respectability.

The point of this contrast is to illustrate that the Lord is too great to be reducible to any mundane characterization based on any one incident. The Lord's activities, known as lila or pastimes, are enacted to serve varying purposes. Accordingly, different pastimes demonstrate different qualities. As Rama, his pastime primarily demonstrated the principle of sacrifice. As Krishna, his pastime primarily demonstrated the principle of compassion.

Inspiration for Selflessness

The Ramayana's extreme examples of selflessness can inspire us to infuse a healthy dose of selflessness into our relationships. Significantly, Indian society that has drawn enduring inspiration from the Ramayana is characterized by robust family relationships. In many parts of the world, families are falling apart. But in India, the family structure is still strong. Much of this strength comes from the readiness of family members to sacrifice for each other.

Appreciating Rama's forsaking Sita as an act of supreme sacrifice harmonizes with the Ramayana's seminal starting question—who was the ideal person? The eponymous epic declares Rama the ideal person. A person who abandons his pregnant wife can hardly be considered ideal. But a person who consistently demonstrates the virtue of selflessness, no matter what it costs him—even if it costs him separation from his pregnant wife—that person is indeed extraordinary. And when both husband and wife demonstrate such selfless spirit, meditating on those exalted exemplars can offer immortal inspiration.

The Ramayana: A Short Summary

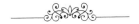

Millennia ago, when a tyrannical demon-king Ravana oppressed the universe, the Supreme Lord descended as Rama to re-establish dharma, moral and spiritual order. Rama appeared in the city of Ayodhya as the son of king Dasharatha, the ruler of the kingdom of Koshala. Dasharatha had three principal queens: Kaushalya, who begot Rama; Sumitra, who begot Lakshmana and Shatrughna; and Kaikeyi, who begot Bharata. All the four brothers grew up happily together, with Rama bonding especially with Lakshmana, and Bharata with Shatrughna. During his youth, Rama displayed peerless prowess in protecting sages from demoniac upstarts. While guarding the fire-sacrifice of the sage Vishwamitra, he felled the demons Tataka and Subahu, and hurled their associate Maricha far away with a single arrow. Maricha, struck with fear, gave up his demonic ways and became an ascetic.

With the blessings of Vishwamitra, Rama won the hand of the princess of Mithila, Sita, in an archery contest, and the two were married in a great celebration. His three brothers simultaneously married a sister of Sita, and two of her cousins. By his noble demeanour and endearing qualities, Rama won the heart of the royal sages, ministers, and citizens of Ayodhya.

In due course of time, Dasharatha decided to appoint Rama as the prince regent. But that plan was disrupted by a political conspiracy—Dasharatha's youngest and favourite wife, Kaikeyi, being instigated by her maid, Manthara, used an old promise of her husband to have Rama exiled to the forest for fourteen years and have her own son Bharata appointed as prince regent. Rama gracefully accepted the banishment and decided to go to the forest, pacifying, as far as he could, the shocked family members, courtiers and citizens. Sita insisted that as his wife she would stick by his side through thick and thin. Lakshmana was incensed at the unfairness of Rama's banishment and initially recommended a coup against the king, but eventually he accepted the sentence and insisted that he too would accompany Rama. Thus, Rama departed for the forest, with Sita and Lakshmana.

Dasharatha was heartbroken at the departure of Rama and soon gave up his life. Bharata, who was not in Ayodhya when all this drama and trauma unfolded, was summoned back by the royal priest, Vashishta, who temporarily took up the responsibility of the administration. Bharata, along with Shatrughna, returned forthwith and was aghast to see that the flourishing city of Ayodhya had become a virtual ghost town. When he came to know what his mother had done, ostensibly for his sake, he was appalled. He censured her for her machinations, and the horror of what she had done registered in Kaikeyi, making her profoundly remorseful.

After performing the last rites of his deceased father, Bharata resolved to go to the forest to beseech Rama to return and take the mantle of kingship. Delighted at his noble resolve, the priests, courtiers and citizens of Ayodhya accompanied him, along with a large regiment of the state army. They met Rama, Lakshmana, and Sita, on the mountain of Chitrakuta, where they were living in a small forest cottage.

When Rama heard the news of his father's demise, he broke down. But recovering his composure, he urged Bharata to responsibly take up the royal responsibility as the king. When Bharata begged him to assume that responsibility, Rama gently but firmly refused. After a long loving argument, Rama finally accepted the kingdom that Bharata offered and entrusted it back to Bharata for the duration of fourteen years so that he could honour his father's word. Reluctantly, Bharata agreed, but he requested Rama to give his sandals, which he would place on the royal throne and on whose behalf he would rule.

Carrying those sandals on his head, the tearful Bharata departed for Ayodhya.

Rama, Lakshmana, and Sita lived in the forest, enriching themselves with spiritual wisdom by associating with the forest sages and learning to relish the simple joy of life close to nature. But Rama also saw the devastation that the cannibalistic demons were wrecking in the forest, desecrating sacrifices, consuming sages, and terrorizing everyone. Ever conscious of his responsibilities as a member of the royal dynasty to protect his citizens, Rama moved deeper into the forest, going southwards till he came to the Dandaka forest, close to where the demons lived. There, they met Jatayu, an aged vulture who had been a friend of Dasharatha and who promised to help protect Sita in the dangerous forest.

While in Dandaka, the demoness Shurapanakha, who was a sister of the demon-king Ravana, became lusty for Rama. Using her shape-shifting abilities, she assumed a beautiful form and propositioned him. When he refused, saying that he was already married to Sita, she felt that Sita was the obstacle to her attainment of Rama and tried to strangle her. The brothers stopped her and let her off with a light punishment for her attempt at assassination—at Rama's command, Lakshmana cut off her nose. Feeling frustrated and humiliated, she complained to her brothers, Khara and Dushana, who were stationed nearby at Janasthana. Infuriated at what they felt was the audacity of mere humans in disfiguring their sister, they swooped down upon Rama along with their commander Trishira and a regiment of fourteen thousand demons. Rama asked Lakshmana to take Sita to the safety of a nearby cave and guard her there. Then, exhibiting astounding prowess, he single-handedly decimated all the demons.

Mad with anger and fear, Shurapanakha fled, wandering aimlessly in the forest, till she finally decided to go to the kingdom of Lanka, where reigned her most powerful brother, Ravana. The demon-king had already been informed of the carnage at Janasthana and had thought of seeking revenge against Rama. Ravana had boons that granted him immunity from gods and other celestial beings, but not from humans. So, he decided against confronting Rama directly, but schemed to abduct his wife and thereby get back at him. When he tried to enlist Maricha into his scheme, for that demon had extraordinary shape-shifting abilities, Maricha warned him that antagonizing Rama was tantamount to courting destruction, for the Ayodhya prince's power was peerless. Chastened, Ravana returned to Lanka.

But when Shurapanakha came to Lanka, gave her own spin to the events at Janasthana and especially when she incited him sexually by describing the beauty of Sita, Ravana became maddened by lust and resolved to abduct Sita. He forced Maricha to join in the conspiracy by threatening him with instant death. Maricha assumed the form of a charming deer and started frolicking near Rama's hermitage. When Sita spotted the deer, her heart was captivated, and she requested Rama to get that deer for her as a pet. But when Rama tried to catch the deer, it sped away, leading Rama deep into the forest, far away from Sita. When Rama finally shot the deer, it transformed into the demon Maricha, who with his last breath impersonated Rama's voice and called out to Lakshmana and Sita for help. Frantic with anxiety for her Lord, Sita urged Lakshmana to go to Rama's aid, goading him with harsh words. Lakshmana, despite being suspicious of a conspiracy, reluctantly departed.

With Sita unguarded, Ravana approached her. Assuming the garb of a mendicant, he got her to lower her guard and then he abducted her. Jatayu fought fiercely to stop the abduction, but the aged bird soon grew tired, and the demon heartlessly lopped off both his wings, and sped away with Sita by the airways. Jatayu survived long enough to inform Rama about Sita's abduction. Rama performed the last rites for the martyr vulture and then started searching for Sita.

During the search, Rama met the tribal lady, Shabari, who lovingly offered him sweet berries that he she had meticulously selected by tasting them. Rama accepted the devotional offering and offered her his supreme grace. Resuming his search, he met the heroic monkey-warrior, Hanuman, who was the minister of the exiled monkey-prince, Sugriva. Sugriva was living in fear of his brother, Vali, who, due to a misunderstanding, had deemed him a traitor. Vali had driven Sugriva out of the kingdom, taken his wife for himself, and had tried repeatedly to kill him. Angered at Vali's atrocious treatment of Sugriva, Rama slew Vali. Before his death, Vali repented, apologized to

Sugriva and requested him to take care of his wife, Tara, and his son, Angada. Sugriva himself was remorseful at the death of his brother and he sorrowfully accepted the responsibility and the throne.

Soon, the rainy season started, bringing with it unusually heavy rains, which made them postpone the search for Sita till the four months of the rainy season ended. During that time, Sugriva, who had been forced to live an austere forest life, lost himself in revelry and forgot all about his promise to aid Rama in finding Sita. But he was reminded in time by Tara and Hanuman—as well as by an indignant Lakshmana who had been sent by Rama to enquire why the search hadn't started even though the rainy season had ended.

His good sense restored, Sugriva competently organized search parties to look for Sita in all the four directions. Hanuman, along with several other powerful monkey-generals, was sent to the south, the direction in which Ravana had been seen to have taken Sita. When the monkeys couldn't find her whereabouts and were about to lose heart, coincidentally, they met a vulture, Sampati, who happened to be the elder brother of Jatayu, and who knew the location of Lanka. When their progress towards Lanka was stalled by the huge ocean at the southern coast, Hanuman, by his supernatural power, jumped across the ocean, braved many dangers, and reached Lanka, the capital of Ravana's kingdom. After an exhaustive search throughout the city, Hanuman finally found Sita, incarcerated and agony-stricken in a palace-garden, and reassured her that Rama would soon come to rescue her. Then, as a part of a reconnaissance strategy for the imminent war, Hanuman battled with the demons to assess their strength. After besting several formidable demons, Hanuman allowed himself to be arrested so that he could meet Ravana face-to-face and deliver him a stern warning on behalf of Rama. When the arrogant Ravana tried to insult and injure Hanuman by burning his tail, the monkey broke free from his shackles and used his burning tail to set ablaze a major part of Lanka. He thus demoralized the enemy forces by this foretaste of the devastation awaiting them in the upcoming war. His mission accomplished, Hanuman jumped back across the ocean and returned to Rama, who after hearing his exploits, embraced him in gratitude and joy.

Heading a massive monkey-army, Rama set off toward Lanka and built a special bridge to cross the ocean. While they were planning to launch an attack on Lanka, Ravana's brother, Vibhishana, joined them. He had tried his best to persuade Ravana to return Sita and avoid a disastrous war, but he had been rebuffed and reviled, leaving him with no option except to go over to Rama's side.

A fierce battle ensued between the poorly-armed forces of Rama and the heavily-armed forces of Ravana, a battle in which the valiant monkeys slowly but surely gained the upper hand. One by one, Ravana sent his generals to the battlefield and Rama's army sent them to death's abode. Even Ravana's gigantic brother, Kumbhakarna, was felled by Rama's unstoppable arrows. Eventually, Ravana's son,

Indrajita, by a deceitful attack, lay low both Rama and Lakshmana as well as most of the monkey-army. To revive them, Hanuman flew to the distant Himalayan mountain ranges and brought back an entire hill that contained the required medicinal herbs. Thus revived, the princes as well as their soldiers started making short work of the demons. Lakshmana felled Indrajita after a long, fierce battle. Aggrieved and enraged, Ravana entered the fray and, after a final, furious confrontation, was slain by Rama.

Rama and Sita were thus reunited and they, along with the monkeys, returned to Ayodhya, where Rama was joyfully coronated as the king. Rama rewarded the monkeys for their heroic services and then they returned back to their kingdoms. Hanuman, however, stayed on in Ayodhya to lovingly serve the beloved Lord of his heart.

While Rama and Sita were living happily in Ayodhya, on the way to expand their family, a horrible rumour alleging Sita's unchastity started spreading throughout the kingdom. Feeling that the rumour was impossible to counter, Rama had Lakshmana send the pregnant Sita to the forest. Though devastated, Sita eventually understood and accepted Rama's decision and found shelter at the hermitage of the sage, Valmiki. There, she had two sons, Lava and Kusha, who grew up to become great heroes, equal to their father.

After giving sufficient time for the rumors to die down, Rama called Sita back. She returned but only to depart from the world by entering into the earth from which she had emerged. Distraught, Rama too departed from the world by going on a journey to the North. Thus, the Divine Couple rose from this mortal realm where they had temporarily descended and became joyfully reunited in their eternal abode, which is the arena of endless divine love.

APPENDIX TWO

The World of
Pure Love

Love is our greatest, deepest need. Our bodies do need air, water, and food, but these bodily needs don't satisfy our desire for loving and being loved. Where does our longing for love come from?

The wisdom literatures of ancient India explain that it comes from our innermost self, our soul. The soul, called in Sanskrit as the *atma*, animates the body just as a driver activates a car. The soul is by its very constitution *sat-cit-ananda*, eternal, full of knowledge, and full of bliss. Bhagavad-gita (15.07) describes that the soul is an eternal fragmental part of God.

The ancient Indian wisdom literatures are a vast body of literatures derived from the Vedas. Vedas are traditionally considered to have divinely co-manifested with the world as a manual for the world, and the body of literatures that follow the Vedic conclusions are referred to as the Vedic texts. Among the most important of the philosophical Vedic texts is the philosophical masterpiece, Bhagavad-gita (known in short as the Gita), which Ralph Waldo Emerson proclaimed as 'the voice of an old intelligence that has pondered and disposed all the questions that exercise us today.' While the Gita, and the Vedanta-Sutra, are the primary metaphysical texts, the Ramayana, along with the Mahabharata, are the primary pastime texts that have attracted millions for millennia. About Ramayana's influence, eminent literary historian A. A. MacDonnell noted: 'Probably no other work of world literature has produced so profound an influence in the life and thought of a people as the Ramayana.'

The Vedic texts reveal God to be much more than the stereotypes of a stern judge or a pliant order-supplier. God, the Vedic texts explain, is an enchanting loving person, replete with all the qualities that attract us to various people in this world. We are attracted to beautiful people; God is supremely beautiful. We are attracted to powerful people; God is supremely powerful. Similarly, God is supremely wise, supremely wealthy, supremely famous, and supremely renounced. Over and above these six excellences, God has a seventh, most endearing excellence—the supremely loving nature. God personally and fully reciprocates love with every single soul. The one God who is known in different religious traditions as Jehovah, Christ, Allah, reveals himself in various eternal forms in His own kingdom. Prominent among those forms are the forms of Rama and Krishna. The names 'Rama' and 'Krishna', though often thought of as referring to Hindu gods, refer etymologically to universal attributes of God. 'Rama' means 'the source of all pleasure', and 'Krishna' refers to 'the all-attractive one.'

In fact, the Vedic revelation of God is even more inclusivist, even more appealing. God manifests himself eternally in two forms: one male and one female. Thus God is not just Rama, but Sita-Rama, where Sita is not just the eternal consort of God, but also God in a female form. Similarly, God is not just Krishna, but Radha-Krishna. The reciprocation of love between the Divine Couple is the original divine romance that goes on eternally in the spiritual realm. All souls share in that divine romance according to their individual spiritual natures.

The Gita (8.20) describes that this wonderful realm of love—called variously as the spiritual world or the kingdom of God—exists far beyond the material world.

God wants all souls to relish fully the joy of loving him. As true love is not possible without freedom, so all souls are endowed with free will. The material world where we presently reside is the place for those souls who unfortunately misuse their free will and choose not to love God, but to try to be God themselves, that is, they try to be the Supreme themselves.

In this world, souls are offered material bodies, which cause them forgetfulness of their spiritual identities and give them pseudo-identities. In this material world, the souls seek substitutes for God—be they people or things or ideas—and repose love in them to find happiness. However, this just doesn't work primarily because having once tasted the sweetness of loving God, nothing else can satisfy the soul's hunger for love. Sadly, the souls rarely realize this and keep chasing one object after another till their bodies grow old, get diseased, and die. Then they are given new bodies according to their desires and activities, and they transmigrate in the cycle of birth and death through the millions of species that populate this world. All of us are among the numerous souls living in forgetfulness of our spiritual treasures.

The Lord, out of his causeless love for all souls, sends his sons, messengers, and messages, to remind us of his love and to invite them back to their original home. However, his love for us is so great that he is not satisfied with these spiritual relief measures. So he himself descends to this world periodically as an avatar to display his world of love and thus attract the forgetful souls to return, just as the trailer of a movie attracts us to watch the full movie. The Sanskrit word 'avatar' is often translated as 'incarnation', but that English word literally means 'to come in flesh.' The Lord, however, does not appear in a material form, but appears in his eternal, spiritual form, and so a more accurate English rendition of 'avatar' is 'descent' or 'divine descent.'

When the Lord descends, he teaches primarily the path of love, also known as bhakti-yoga, to help souls regain their spiritual rights to an eternal, joyful life. The word 'bhakti' refers to the sentiment of love, especially when it is directed to God. And the word 'yoga' refers to the process that links the soul with God. (The bodily postures that are popularly known as yoga are one stage of one type of process to connect with God.) Thus bhakti-yoga, also known in short as bhakti, is not a sectarian Hindu process, but is the universal essence of all the theistic religions of the world. All these great religions declare their ultimate perfection to be developing the practitioner's love for God, which is the purpose of bhakti-yoga too.

The Vedic bhakti tradition explains that bhakti-yoga is much more than an isolated activity done occasionally in a life filled with worldly preoccupations, which is the notion about religion among most people—even most religious people. Bhakti-yoga introduces us to a worldview and a culture that integrates and harmonizes the apparently material aspects of our life with the spiritual purpose of life.

Thus, in bhakti-yoga, we learn to see our family spiritually as God's family, as comprising of God's beloved children entrusted to our care. Thus we can develop our love for God by loving and serving our family members and helping them develop their love for God. In this way, bhakti-yoga dramatically transforms our vision of our self-interest. By material calculations, we lose when we have to serve others except for the future gain we may get if they reciprocate with our service. But by devotional calculations, we gain, here and now, by serving others because that service awakens our love for God in our own hearts, irrespective of whether they reciprocate or not. Thus bhakti-yoga, by freeing us from being dependent on others' responses, helps bring the best from within us, which in turn inspires others to bring out their best.

Similarly, bhakti-yoga enables us to see our profession spiritually, as an arena where we can develop our love for God by using our talents and energies to help make the world a better place so that everyone can learn to love him. With this vision, we understand that irrespective of whether our specific projects succeed or not, we keep succeeding in life's ultimate project as long as we keep trying our best. This reassurance of our spiritual success frees us from the stress and anxiety that weakens and cripples so many people today due to the uncertainty of their material success. And, paradoxically, the more we are freed by our spirituality from dependence on material success, the more we can focus our energies on giving our best performance, thus increasing the probability of that success.

Many people fear that if they become spiritual, then they will not be able to perform in the material sphere. In bhakti-yoga, the more spiritual we become, the better we can be materially, because our spirituality gives us a vision and purpose that empowers us to function in the material sphere without being dependent on its dualities and its uncertainties.

In this way, bhakti-yoga paves the way to the culture of loving service.

Acknowledgements

My first thanks to my many spiritual mentors, especially HH Bhakti Rasamrita Maharaj, HH Jayadvaita Maharaj, and HH Radhanath Maharaj—their blessings are the engine for my writing.

My next thanks to my friends who helped in reviewing and improving the content, Avatari Chaitanya P, Muralidhar P, Revati Vallabha P, Manish Vithalani P, and Trivikrama P.

My heartfelt thanks to the competent and committed team at Fingerprint! Publishing that edited the book and designed the cover image.

Many others helped in various ways.

My heartfelt thanks to them all.

Chaitanya Charan is a mentor, life coach, and monk. Building on his engineering degree from the Government College of Engineering, Pune, he complemented his scientific training with a keen spiritual sensitivity. For over two decades, he has researched ancient wisdom texts and practised their teachings in a living yoga tradition.

Author of over twenty-five books, he writes the world's only Gita-daily feature (gitadaily.com), wherein he has penned over two thousand daily meditations on the Bhagavad-gita. Known for his systematic talks and incisive question-answer sessions, he has spoken on motivational and spiritual topics across the world at universities such as Stanford, Princeton, and Cambridge, and companies such as Intel, Microsoft, and Google.